The Montessori Mission

10 Montessorians Communities Questions Perspectives

The Montessori Mission is a project of passion, birthed from a deep desire to showcase the breadth, depth, diversity and inclusivity that Montessori offers (but, unfortunately, isn't always reflected in the stereotypical image of a Montessori setting). Conceived originally as a 10-episode Podcast Series, evolved into a book, thanks to the phenomenal support and guidance of the Podcast guests, who without their generosity in sharing their wisdom, knowledge and insight, this project would not have been possible. The magic in this book comes from them, and their willingness to share their deep and fascinating lived experiences. I am deeply grateful.

Montessori Educator, Parenting Mentor, Podcast Host, Author and Big Dreamer - Charlotte supports parents and Educators on their path of raising and guiding capable, caring, contributors, so that each of us can play our unique part in creating a more peaceful, just, and harmonious world for all. Her vision is underpinned by the pioneering work of visionary Educator Dr Maria Montessori, nurturing the natural development of each child—physical, emotional and spiritual. Charlotte lives in Dubai with her two young children, where she seeks to live a life of passion and purpose; transforming Montessori from an alternative education to a mainstream way of life— for the upliftment and nourishment of all beings.

www.enrichingenvironments.com

For Olivia and Harry,
and all of the children I have had the
honour of guiding.

The Montessori Mission, by Charlotte Awdry

Contents

My love letter to the world.

I first knew that I wanted to write a book about Montessori seven years ago shortly after my daughter, Olivia, was born. In February 2015, when she was seven weeks old I put together a vision board, and one of the cards on this board read 'bestselling author'. The title of that book was called 'Ten Things I Want My Humans To Know', and was based upon a piece of work I completed for my Introduction to Assistants to Infancy course that I did in collaboration with the Association Montessori Internationale (AMI)[1] and the Sustainability Institute at Lynedoch[2], just outside of Cape Town.

Undertaking such an intensive and introductory course whilst I was pregnant with Olivia was a humbling experience, and it gave me an insight into the type of human I wanted to become and how I wanted to give, serve, and uplift others. Our AMI trainer, Julia Hilson, spoke of her work in diverse communities all over the world and described how gaining the trust of every child that comes into our care, and learning to trust each child to unfold in their own time, is the key work of an Educator.

Sharing this learning space with women from a variety of backgrounds, from all over South Africa, left a beautiful imprint on my heart. Each woman was dedicated to the raising, and raising up of our littlest children, with dignity and respect. I look back at my three years in Cape Town and am now able to understand how this profound experience shaped me.

I have known since I was a teenager that I wanted to contribute and serve in some way, but for many years did not know how to put this into practice. Throughout my twenties I searched for a way to bring meaning, but did not have the tools at my disposal to know which direction to take. I had a variety of fun and adventurous careers, working in IT in California during the dot-com boom, and then in travel on the Cote d'Azur. For a time I owned a cheese shop in Cheltenham, UK with my then partner, led wine tours around the world, and yoga holidays in Europe. Montessori came into my world in 2010 when I picked up a Montessori International magazine and was instantly captivated with what I read. Looking back, I can see that my fascination with this magazine set me on this path of self-discovery. By early 2011 it seemed that everyone I spoke to had a link to

The Montessori Mission, by Charlotte Awdry

Montessori in some way! I took this as a clue to what I was searching for, so took myself to an Open Day at Montessori Centre International in London; I signed up for the 3-6 course that same day. I was fascinated and excited to have at last found an intellectual challenge and a new direction.

However, as the start date for the course approached, the voices of doubt started ringing in my ears: "I don't know if this is what I really want to do... Maybe it won't challenge me enough... Do I even want to teach?"

How wrong I was. Once I was in, I was all in. I began my Montessori journey at the age of 34. I quickly learnt that in a Montessori environment the Guide's focus is on being with the child and guiding them, I wasn't really teaching anyone anything! And the spiritual preparation that is called of us as Montessori Educators and parents has challenged and continues to challenge me beyond what I thought was possible.

After completing my Teaching Practice I was hungry to practice Montessori overseas, so my then husband and I decided to embark upon an adventure. We pulled out an atlas and chose South Africa as our destination. My experience of teaching in Cape Town could not have been more different from my Teaching Placement in the affluent Borough of Islington in London. And it significantly shaped my understanding of Montessori in the context of social justice. In Cape Town, the children in my class were different ethnicities and from very different socio-economic groups, but they were all having similar positive outcomes. There were children from townships and children of famous South African actors in my class, and when they came together in the classroom these differences did not come into play. There was joy, there was creativity, there was community, there was safety, and there was learning. What I had read about and heard about during my studies was true: this educational method could be a pathway to a more peaceful, just and harmonious world.

We moved to Dubai when Olivia was seven months old, and had our second child Harry, in 2017. In 2018 Enriching Environments was born. It started as a grassroots Montessori Toddler Community ; families who were coming to my home for a weekly storytime session started asking questions about why my artwork was displayed at a child's height on the wall, why Harry spent all of his time cleaning the windows or mopping the floor, and why everyone slept on mattresses on the floor rather than in beds! I coached each family on preparing their homes in a Montessori way and week by week each family rotated hosting the group in their houses; it truly was a special time, creating this community from scratch. It was also a huge time of growth for all of us; our early core group of Hani, Oscar, Olivia and Harry taught us so much, like the importance of involving toddlers in food preparation, supporting children with biting, having free indoor and outdoor access if possible, and how cleaning is often the dominant interest for the 1-3 age group! Time went by, our confidence grew, our group expanded and more families joined us.

During the COVID pandemic in 2020 we were not able to continue with the group, so I used this time to build a social media presence and created a Montessori-at-home self-study course online, to share our Enriching Environments journey with other parents. When Olivia and Harry both started attending an authentic Montessori school[3] here in Dubai in January 2021, I shifted to a more Consultancy focus, working with more families one-on-one in their homes, and hosted more Workshops both in person and online.

In April 2021 I hosted an online writing project for the month of Ramadan with my friend Noora Hefzi (IG:@noorahefzi) with the vision of completing a book by Eid al-Fitr. This required me to write for 15 minutes every day for 30 days, which I dedicated myself to. And although I did not complete a book, the project triggered my creativity and from this intensely creative time the idea for The Montessori Mission Podcast came to life.

The idea to turn the Podcast series into a book came from my guest from Episode 1. I first met Jeanne-Marie in August 2020 at the Montessori Everywhere (IG: @montessorieverywhere150) online event in celebration of Dr Montessori's 150th birthday. We were together in one of the discussion breakout rooms and found an instant connection. We kept in touch and were discussing a possible project together when the idea of the Podcast came to me. Jeanne-Marie agreed to be the first guest on the series and has been a great cheerleader and confidante throughout the process. She has the innate gift of offering the perfect piece of guidance at exactly the right time!

As I reflect back on the growth I have experienced during a decade in Montessori and seven years as a mother, I can see how Dr Montessori's vision of a more peaceful and harmonious world has resonated with me deeply and persistently when things were tough. Since finding Montessori, I have always known at my core that this work was meant for me. And although there have been points in my life where I questioned myself, and my abilities, I knew at my core that Montessori is my passion, that it was my vehicle to grow, to empower others and to serve.

Preparing for the Enriching Environments Toddler Community sessions became like a meditation for me; there were many days when, due to mental health issues I was experiencing, I did not have the strength to get out of bed, however, the rhythm and stability in preparing the space for the children I was welcoming that day allowed me to access an inner courage that I didn't know that I had. I

The Montessori Mission, by Charlotte Awdry

developed a deep understanding of the power of the prepared environment for the child as they step into the classroom every day—how the child draws a sense of calm and inner strength from the sacredness of this ordered and beautiful space.

So, this book, this love letter to the world, has been seven years in the making. There have been a few hiccups and false starts along the way, and the title of the book has changed, although it still has the theme of 10 in it!

I seek for this to be a manual of how to be human; for parents, caregivers, Educators and students to gain and/or develop their understanding of how we can all contribute to a more peaceful and harmonious world. When being with or working with young children, the hours are long and invariably the pay is poor; however, know that you have the power to create a new world, a more just and fair world. So, to fellow parents and caregivers, your work is invaluable. Thank you all.

I hope that everyone who picks up this book finds something within the lived experiences of my guests that resonates with their story, culture and background.

I acknowledge the privilege that I was born with and offer heartfelt thanks to all 10 of my guests who have shared their stories and hearts so generously; Educators with so much more knowledge, wisdom and experience than I have. Thank you for your trust in me, and I deeply appreciate how you have all encouraged and supported me in this passion project, showing a more diverse and rounded spectrum of the limitless possibilities for Montessori Education and Montessori Parenting.

Love deeply in all that you do.

Charlotte

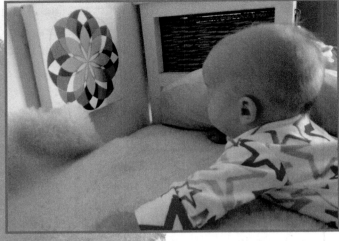

Images: From top, left to right
(1) End of exams at Montessori Centre International, London, 2012 **(2)** Harry, 3 mths – he would spend up to half an hour gazing at patterns, this mandala was his favourite **(3)** Left to right, Simon, Tanaka, Isha, Siya – Little Hands Montessori, 2013 **(4)** The view of Devil's Peak from our house in Observatory , Cape Town **(5)** With Olivia at the Waterfront – Cape Town April 2015 **(6)** First time I held Harry at two days old, March 2017

Images: From top to bottom
(1) Classroom at Little Hands Montessori Cape Town, September 2013
(2) Yoga with elephants at Bakubung Bush Lodge, South Africa, September 2013
(3) The original Enriching Environments Community, October 2018

Reflective practices

What are they, and how do you use them?

My invitation with the Reflective Practices that complete each chapter is to guide us all into a deeper understanding of our child, the children in our care, and ourselves.

There is no right or wrong way of approaching the practices. Some elements may seem more appealing than others at different times. Some chapters may speak to you and your current path as a parent, caregiver or Educator, and some not. Sometimes where we feel most resistance can be where our greatest capacity for growth is, so it can be interesting to feel into any resistance by identifying and locating the sensations that arise in our body. As ever, tuning into our bodies' messages and what feels right is safe guidance. Our bodies carry their own innate wisdom of what we are ready for in the next stage of our growth.

1. Journalling

Journalling can be one of many gateways into becoming familiar with our inner landscape. There is power in writing down our thoughts, questions and challenges. Journalling looks different for everyone; for some, it is a simple act of writing out the question or challenge, and allowing the answers to rise from within, without any further writing. For others, the writing itself is the process, as journalling becomes a way to express our feelings on paper, and we can actually see our process, development and growth unfold in front of our eyes. My journey with journalling started a decade ago during my 3-6 Montessori Diploma; daily journalling was an integral part of the reflective practice of the in-classroom Practical Training element of the Diploma, which takes place after having completed the theory. In these Reflective Practices I invite you into the transformational growth that can unfold from journalling.

2. Embodiment

My understanding of embodiment and how it has unfolded on my healing journey is the ability for us to feel into our bodies, to feel what is there, the sensations that arise with our emotions, without the story behind them.

Young children are naturally embodied because they express how they are feeling in the moment; they do not suppress their feelings or joy or discomfort, in the same way that adults have learnt to. As they do not have the linguistic capacity to explain their upset, frustration or overwhelm, they unconsciously express it through their bodies in the form of screaming, crying, or having a tantrum. When they are in safe spaces with adults who allow them to express their full range of emotions, they naturally release all they need to, and do not hold onto the stress afterwards.

It feels to me that allowing ourselves to once again connect deeply with our bodies is the missing piece. When it comes to our intuition, inner guidance system, insight and wisdom, as is within the wisdom of our body—our work is simply to believe in it, and then learn to access it.

My invitation is for us to reconnect with our bodies, allowing ourselves to feel all that is there, even when we are far beyond early childhood, and guide our children in maintaining this connection with their bodies.

These practices of feeling rather than seeking fix or rationalise can seem alien and confronting at times. Statements that we heard from adults such as 'You need to finish the food on your plate' seemed normal a generation ago, however listening to our body's intelligence starts from the earliest years. It seems a very simplistic example, however knowing when we are feeling satisfied and have had enough to eat is a part of coming to understand what feels good to us. Insisting that a child continue eating or finish their plate when they are no longer hungry demands that they override their body's wisdom. We send them a message that complying with our wishes is more important than acting upon their body's intelligence.

When practising connecting with your bodily sensations and inviting your child into doing the same you might consider following these simple steps:

Lie next to your child at night before they fall asleep, invite them to close their eyes and deepen their breath, inhaling for a count of four and exhaling for a count of four. As they begin to relax, you can draw their attention to how they feel in their bodies by placing one hand on their heart and one on their belly.

Reflective practices

Focus on simple concepts like tuning into and asking the question:
'What feels good right now?' The blankets around us keeping us cosy? Our bodies sinking into the mattress? The sense of being together as a family at the end of the day?

A second practice is to explore sensations in the body associated with strong emotions. Verbalising how different events feel in their body. An example might be "My heart felt so full and bursting with love when we were running in the waves and playing on the beach, it was such fun."

Often times with negative emotions we jump to logic, reasoning, blame of others or ourselves. An invitation is to pause when experiencing a negative emotion, identifying where it is located in the body, its colour and texture.

We can do the same when our child is having a tough time; having a tantrum, complaining or being defiant. Are we able to pause before responding and experience the sensations within our bodies first? What is the colour of that sensation, and the texture? My difficult emotions are often thick, black and sticky.

We also invite our child into this practice of leaning into their bodily sensations through our role modelling. We verbalise our heavier emotions, "I felt so shaky when the gentleman shouted at me in the traffic jam, my heart was racing and my tummy was really gurgling, it didn't feel good."

After an upset, a tantrum, an argument with a friend, invite your child into getting familiar with the landscape of their inner world:

'I saw what was happening on the outside of your body when you were frustrated with your brother, your fists were clenched; I wonder what was happening inside your body, what did you feel and where did you feel it?'

This practice can be expanded to serve as a tool as part of a healing process; for example following the death of a grandparent or family pet, a close friend moving overseas, a difficult time at school or with friends, moving house.

The Montessori Mission, by Charlotte Awdry

Whenever your child speaks of their sadness, anger or frustration, gently encourage them to lean into the full spectrum of these emotions. Talk through locating bodily sensations, the colour, the texture, allow whatever is there to be there, no matter how painful. Develop this into a soothing ritual as needed.

When they have expressed all they need to about their feelings or sensations you can invite them into a heart healing practice. Lie close to your child and place your hand on their heart, invite them to do the same on yours. Breathe love from your heart into theirs slowly and deeply; visualise the depth of your love flowing to them. Our intention is to literally 'blast' our child with love! Offering the gift of a safe container to feel all that they are feeling without judgement, without having to hide it from us, and without us invalidating their feelings by telling them they are 'fine'.

Giving our children (and thus ourselves) permission to truly feel, and to express whatever is within is courageous work, and offers us a way to process all that we experience, the natural ups and downs of life.

My personal experience of this approach with Olivia and Harry has been a humbling journey of self-reflection. After their father and I divorced and he then left Dubai to return to the UK, it was deeply painful to see in vivid colour their confusion, and sense of loss at his departure. The beautiful practice as detailed above became our soothing ritual to process and integrate the storm of emotions felt during that time. One that I hope has given them the space to feel seen, heard and comforted; and offers them resilience in the long term.

Learning to gently lean into our difficult emotions and modelling this to our children cultivates empathy, acceptance and compassion for self and others. It feels to me, that this is another path we can follow to contribute to creating a more peaceful and harmonious world. People that are deeply connected to themselves and their inner landscape naturally seek to connect to others in the same way; we are able to see the fragility and vulnerability of all of humanity mirrored from ourselves to others. The Buddhist practice of *ahimsa* (to do no harm), a practice reflected in many world religions, feels resonant as we navigate our own personal growth.

My reflection

3. Creativity

Barbara Isaacs (Chapter 5) gave me the idea to include children in the Creativity Reflective Practice, as an opportunity to connect deeper with them in their experience. So this part of the Reflective Practice is for your play, your imagination, your big dreams and visions: a chance to ignite your fire of creativity and have fun in the process.

So much of our lives in Western society is formulaic and transactional; we are programmed to do more, achieve more, consume more. Creativity (unless we are in a creative profession) seems a luxury.

A forgotten truth is that our desire to create for the sake of creativity is one of the unique qualities that we possess as humans. Creativity invites us into the full spectrum of experiencing life through all of our senses.

Through the Creative Practices in this book, I seek to evoke joy and playfulness into the serious business of parenting, childcare and education.

The Montessori Mission, by Charlotte Awdry

Land acknowledgements

I have included land acknowledgements, where applicable, as a way of celebrating Indigenous culture and recognising the long-standing history that comes with residing on colonised land.

Trish Moquino from Cochiti Pueblo in New Mexico (Chapter 4) offers us a deep understanding of the attempted erasure of Indigenous communities since the arrival of European settlers in North America.

The Reflective Practices for Chapter 4 invite us into exploring the cultural heritage of the land on which we reside.

Jeanne-Marie Paynel

Born in Tunisia, spending her childhood between France and the United States; Jeanne-Marie now lives in San Diego, United States, on the original land of the Kumeyaay people.

Jeanne-Marie has had a passion for babies and young children throughout her life. She found Montessori, or Montessori found her, when she was pregnant with her first child.

After qualifying as a Montessori Guide, from speaking to the parents of children in her classrooms, she realised that they were all asking for further guidance of what they could do at home to support their children. These parents were seeing how much their children were thriving in this beautiful, peaceful community at school, and they wanted to bring these values to their home environments. Following many years in the classroom, she has come to her current vision and role as a Parenting Mentor, giving her gifts to the world through mindfulness, minimalism and Montessori.

Jeanne-Marie and I have never met in person, only through Zoom, which I guess is normal life in the world we are living in today, but she is one of those people with the magical quality of making you feel at ease when you first speak to her. She has a big heart, with so much experience and insights to share.

We begin the 10 Questions...

Jeanne-Marie:

My passion is to empower parents, so they are able to parent with confidence and with knowledge. My training in Montessori was so rich in information and encouraged us to follow our own instincts and trust that our children would show us the way. I think it is so important to remind ourselves of that. Montessori does that for us, at least it did for me. I discovered Montessori 25 years ago. My daughter is going to be 25 this summer. I just picked up one book, L'enfant, which is translated as, The Discovery of Childhood (Dr Maria Montessori, 1909). This book was such an eye-opener for what my child needed and what I had to expect in becoming a parent. It really gave me that tool which is so important in observation, to trust ourselves and to trust our child.

I really entered parenting that way, trusting that my child would show me what she needed me to be, who she needed me to be, and what she needed from me.

I had wanted to be a mother for a long time and became a mother later than I had planned. I was just so enthralled with following this little human being who was discovering the world. I know you work with toddlers a lot and you talk about their wonder, their excitement just to feel the wind in their face for the first time. You get to re-experience all of that with your child, and it's beautiful.

It was not until she was eight years old that I had a second child and left my corporate career as a graphic designer, then went back to school to do a Master's in Montessori Education. It is the best thing I ever did—people probably thought I was crazy at the time. At one point I did wonder, when I ended up in a classroom with 25 little humans, "What am I doing here?" I had gone up the ranks in the corporate world and I had traded a private office for a stool in a room full of children. At one point I was like, "Oh my gosh, I am crazy!" But they taught me so much. Teaching in a model classroom at a training centre, it's all behind one-way windows, so we had a lot of parents always observing. When I would walk out into the hallway, they were always mesmerised. "Oh my gosh, they clean up, they prepare food, they're being social." They were full of questions, "What can I do at home? Why is my child acting this way?" They were really taken aback by how different their child was in the Montessori environment than they were at home. What I realised is that parents don't have the information that we have as trained guides, and that has been my mission. This is important, valuable information that every parent on the planet needs to have.

If we want to evolve as a society, if we want to evolve as humanity, if we want to have peace on planet Earth, it is through education and it starts with parents because they are the ones raising the next generation.

Just the other day, I was talking to somebody and she said that the work that all of us are doing with children is not only affecting them, but affecting seven generations to come. That is big work. I have always said my mission is peace on earth, but I'm doing it my way, working with children and their parents.

Charlotte:

It is like demystifying their children for them. They seem like a mystery, these gorgeous little bundles of energy, fire, drive, and determination. We are able to unpick this and demystify it for parents so they can, as you say, learn to observe and trust their inner wisdom. The work is evolving humanity.

Jeanne-Marie:

More importantly to me, it is always just reminding them that they were once children themselves, I think we forget that. In our hearts we are still children. Self-development always comes back to childhood, to those first experiences, and often, it is working on your inner child. It always comes back to what Dr. Montessori (1949), coined as 'The Absorbent Mind'. Those first six years are everything, they are the foundation. That is why I put so much focus on working with expectant parents and parents of young children, because that's really where there is going to be the understanding that this child that we have is also an adult in the making. We have to change our perception of who this human being is.

I do some volunteer doula work and it is just such beautiful work to be able to be in the presence of this divine being. Just seeing this newborn who is a few minutes old, her eyes looking around, here is another opportunity. They come to us so hungry, so ready to know everything, but so pure and that is the pureness I want parents to remember in their own hearts.

1. What does Montessori mean to you?

Jeanne-Marie:

For me, Montessori has been the understanding of human development, a guide to understanding our children's needs, our human needs; a concrete and very uncomplicated, very simple way of understanding human development. This understanding that the newborn child, even the child in utero, comes to us ready to soak in information, to be guided. It is more than a way of educating, it is really a way of life. It is a way of understanding life and understanding human development with these beautiful tools of observation, understanding that children, like I said, come to us so willing, so rich, so pure. It is our role to guide them along. The only difference is that we have just been on planet earth a little longer than they have.

If we can see ourselves as equals to them, to really be there to guide them and say, "Hey, let me show you, I discovered this while you were getting ready to come." I think it just simplifies it and makes it so much richer. It takes away a lot of the stress and the overwhelm that I feel parents have these days.

Charlotte:

Just the simplicity of understanding what their child needs, the basic needs, understanding and allowing our child to experience the joy and the wonder of the world. We can show our children the joy and the wonder of the world. Equally, we receive this gift of being able to experience the joy and the wonder of the world through them.

2. What was your first light bulb moment on your Montessori journey?

Jeanne-Marie:

I think it was that very day when my life took a big turn. I had been a graphic designer for over 20 years, working in advertising in both Paris and here in San Diego where I had moved with my family. We were contemplating moving back to Europe and I did not feel satisfied pitching myself as a graphic designer. I really had to have a conversation with myself, "What do you want to do?" It came back to the children because ever since I was a young teenager, I have always delighted in being in the presence of children. All of my volunteer jobs as a young teenager were in day-cares or children's museums. That's when I called the Montessori Institute here in San Diego and they told me to come in the next morning to meet the Director. That moment when I hung up the phone, I knew that my life was going to take a big turn. My mother had already passed a few years before that and I remember calling a friend of hers and crying - it was like a message that something big was going to happen, to follow my heart. So, I calmed down and went in at 8:00am that morning to meet the Director. She asked me, "Why are you here? Why have you come?" I said,

"I really believe that children are way more capable than we give them credit for."

She looked at me and went: "You have come to the right place." But the real a-ha for me was in the lecture she gave which happened to be about the natural development and freedom of movement that we give to the Montessori child. As I was listening to the lecture, I realised that I had done that for my children without knowing, I had followed that instinct. Thank goodness to that one book I read.

When we lived in Paris, we lived on the fifth storey of an apartment building with no elevator, and my daughter would wrangle out of my arms to climb up those five flights of stairs. She wasn't walking yet but she was determined I would let her do it.

In that lecture, that was the light bulb, "Yes. This is what it's all about, it really is about following the child," and that was a big a-ha for me.

Charlotte:
Your lucky daughter having all of that amazing movement, climbing up those stairs, that's incredible.

Jeanne-Marie:
Five flights of stairs was a lot. I had to be patient, I had to wait. I would sometimes go ahead of her to drop off the groceries and come back down and wait for her. But I could see this enthusiasm, commitment, and determination that she had that was so important.

3. In what ways does Montessori enrich the families that you work with and, hence, the wider community?

Jeanne-Marie:
For me, it is permission to follow your instincts. I had a big a-ha very early when I decided to offer home consultations. I remember going to the home of a family who had an 18-month-old. Only the mom and the boy were home that day; we were looking around in the kitchen, and she said, "I really would like to give him the peeler and zucchinis because he just seems so eager to help." I said, "Of course, yes. That is just perfect." I remember this look on her face of relief that she could, and I realised at that moment that I was giving that encouragement to her to follow her instincts. Families need that love and encouragement that you have in your heart. It might not be a maternal or paternal instinct, but it is remembering what our child wants at that moment.

My mission in working with parents is helping them let go of the overwhelm, stress, and restriction that they need to be the perfect parent. Just enjoy this moment. This is a miraculous time in your life, in your child's life. Be present, follow your child, and re-learn. This is a new opportunity for you to rewire certain things and take advantage of it.

Charlotte:
If we are open to it, we can have our own journey of self-discovery, particularly with young children; there is nowhere to hide because they are there all the time.

Jeanne-Marie:
It is not always easy and I will be perfectly clear about that. For some of us it might

trigger the wounded child within us, it might bring up traumas that we had forgotten. But it is also an opportunity to clear some of that up. You have a brand new, clean, pure, loving heart in front of you, let them guide you, put all the other stuff behind. Those were the cards that you were dealt, but let's deal them a new set of cards, and use that as an opportunity to clear those up.

Charlotte:

That is so profound; we can be the bridge with our child. You said earlier, "We are healing seven generations forward," and recently I've read that when we work on our own stuff, we heal seven generations behind. As you said, in terms of evolution, we can be the bridge at a really strange time in the world for a lot of people. There is so much healing to be had, and if we can let go and be in the present moment, then magic can happen.

Jeanne-Marie:

Exactly. The only way we can do that is to really follow our children because they are in the present moment. There is no other moment for them, they are right here, right now. We should really follow that lead as Dr. Shefali, in The Conscious Parent (2010), says that our children should be our little buddhas. If we can let go of our ego that tells us it has to be this way or that way and be here right now with them—it makes it so much more joyful and miraculous.

4. When was the first time a child taught you something about yourself that you weren't aware of?

Jeanne-Marie:

When I was in training, I was in a three to six classroom and working with a four-year-old girl. We were doing something, and I said, very lovingly, "Yes, sweetie." The little girl replied: "I'm not sweetie. My name is Charlotte." I remember her very strong will, she put a mirror up to me that I had been disrespectful. We are taught to be in the presence of the divine, to be prepared adults, to be in their presence, and she reminded me that I was not being that. It was so pure, so strong. I apologised and said, "Of course, yes, your name is Charlotte. I'm sorry, I should not call you sweetie." It just made total sense. I call everybody my love and my children, but this was not my child.

Charlotte:

That was her boundary. How powerful it is when a four-year-old knows their boundaries like that. That's what I see with the children I work with, and with my own. Their boundaries are rock solid from a very young age and that is really powerful.

Jeanne-Marie:

It is so important that you say that because I think an adult might see it as rude. We should learn from children to set boundaries for ourselves and respect that this is an adult in the making who is saying, "Wait a minute, my name is not sweetie, you need to call me by my name." How wonderful that she was able to do that.

Charlotte:

How powerful. As you said earlier, if we are going to create a new world, if we are raising consciously, if we are evolving, then we need different types of people who are going to stand up to big corporations, stand up against injustices that we see in the world, unfairness and fight for social equality. We need to respond differently and we need to have children who are very strong in their boundaries.

5. When was the last time a child taught you something about yourself that you weren't aware of?

Jeanne-Marie:

I am learning every day. Just being in the presence of a birthing child yesterday was amazing. It wasn't about me as an individual, but how we have a new opportunity every time, just the delight in the parents welcoming their child. I'm just blown away by how the birthing world has evolved and how the fathers have evolved. Every birth that I have gone to, the fathers of the children are so attentive, so loving and very present in the moment. This father was such a delight. At one point I said to him, "You are just a marvellous doula. I don't need to be here," because he was so attentive to being there for her, it was just beautiful. We are evolving in a good way.

6. When was the last time a child caught you out of integrity and questioned you on it?

Jeanne-Marie:

Oh, my goodness! My own children have a way of saying, "Yes, but mom you don't always do it this way." My son is pretty good at saying, "But you promised." It makes me rethink if I really said that. You have to keep your word to yourself and keep your word to them. I think it is so important for us to lower our ego, really hear what they have to say and question our own integrity. They might have a point, sometimes they don't because they are just trying to get away with something, but we have to say, "You are doing a really good job, you have a good argument, I love you and the answer is still no." They put a mirror up to you, for you to re-evaluate how you have been handling a situation, whether it is with yourself, your friends, or your children. It is important for us to be honest with ourselves because we tend to go into defensive mode, "I'm the

The Montessori Mission, by Charlotte Awdry

adult here, I know what I'm talking about." But we don't always know and it is okay to admit that your child might have a point.

7. How did you explain yourself when you were out of integrity?

Jeanne-Marie:

It is very important for us to be able to tell our child, "I've made a mistake. I'm learning each day alongside you and I'm going to make some mistakes, you are going to make some mistakes. All these mistakes are opportunities for us to learn to do better next time." To be able to admit to a child, whether they are your child or somebody else's child, "I am learning, I am a human being, I make mistakes, I am sorry, I am trying to do better every day. I might need your help in doing that." That is so important in the humility of being okay with making mistakes. I make mistakes every day and it's okay. We learn from them, that's how we grow. I think if we can model that to our children, it is going to help them in the world because we tend to be such perfectionists, wanting to get everything right, we get ulcers over it, and it's just not worth it.

Charlotte:

So true. It's a Western society phenomenon as well. Other societies don't have this obsession with perfectionism in the same way that we do. When we practise humility this gives our children the gift of self-compassion, we are able to demonstrate this so powerfully to them. We can show our children from a very young age that when we make a mistake, we're not berating ourselves, we're not beating ourselves up, we're not blaming ourselves. We take responsibility but we know that we are learning, evolving and doing the best we can. Everyone is doing the best they can at that time. That feels like a quantum leap—to apologise to our children is a quantum leap of a generation.

8. What is your favourite Dr. Montessori quote at the moment?

Jeanne-Marie:

I have a hundred favourites. The last time we talked I shared a different one from what I am going to share with you today. It relates more to the work that I do, and it says, "We must help the child to act for himself, will for himself, think for himself. This is the art of those who aspire to serve the spirit." It is taken from Education for a New World [1]. We get an opportunity every time we are in the presence of children to see things differently, to give them the tools to act for themselves, to exercise their will. How often do I work with parents who tell me, "Oh, my child is strong-willed." I say, "That's wonderful, you are so lucky, you have a child who knows what they want in life, that is wonderful." I do feel that I aspire to serve the spirit of a loving, peaceful humanity.

Charlotte:

Serving the spirit. That is just amazing, wonderful.

9. What is your deepest desire for Montessori in the future?

Jeanne-Marie:

I would love to see all ministries of education around the world integrate Montessori principles in modern-day education.

Education, as a whole, needs to be completely revamped. We are on a 19th-century model while in the 21st century; we need to really take it apart and rebuild it for future generations that are being asked to solve a lot of problems.

Our children are going to be asked to really think outside the box, and for that they are going to need tools of adaptation. I really believe that we need to get away from this factory system; churning out good little workers is no longer what we need. We are seeing that the new child coming to us is expanded in so many different ways, we need to prepare ourselves much better for Montessori to be integrated into education all over the world. We also need to work deeper into understanding what our children really need from us. I see it evolving. It's taking time but it was just 100 years ago and we are progressively going. If we can just keep that vision of integrating the tools that she gave us into modern-day education for everyone, it will be great progress for humanity.

10. What do you see is your role in achieving this desire?

Jeanne-Marie:

I intend to continue doing the work that I do—empowering parents to learn to observe their child, to really learn to follow their child, to advocate for their child's education. I work with a lot of families who don't have their children in Montessori schools, or they might be homeschooling. But I try to empower them as much as possible to have the tools to go back to their schools, ask questions, and not take everything they say at face value, and to really advocate for their children and for themselves. The work that I do is bringing peace to the home because that's where world peace starts, at home with our own children. If we can have peaceful, joyful, calm families, we are on our way to a better world. I do that one family at a time and that is my contribution.

Pour une naissance sans violence, an ode to birth itself.

BY FRÉDÉRICK LEBOYER[2]

Nous demandions:
"Comment préparer l'enfant ? Faut-il, avec de fines électrodes…"
Nous nous sentions perdus.
Ce n'est pas l'enfant qu'il faut préparer.
C'est nous.
Ce sont "nos" yeux qu'il faut ouvrir.
C'est "notre" aveuglement qui doit cesser.
Avece seulement un peu d'intelligence,
comme tout pourrait être simple.

English translation:

We asked:
"How to prepare the child? Do we need delicate electrodes…"
We felt lost.
It is not the child we must prepare.
It is us.
It is 'our' eyes we must open.
It is 'our' blindness that must stop.
With just a bit of intelligence,
how everything could be simple.

Jeanne-Marie: I chose this author and passage because it reminds us of our work as Montessorians, it is our preparation that we should concern ourselves with, not the children's. Children come to us ready to learn joyfully so with a bit of intelligence and spiritual preparation we can simply guide them.

A peek into the world of Jeanne-Marie

This page
(1) What I love to do, Private Mentoring

Right-hand page, left to right

(1) When I worked in the Primary classroom at the Montessori Institute of San Diego model classroom
(2) Centuries old Tunisian artistry
(3) Couscous made by my father, keeping our North African roots alive
(4) Henri Cartier-Bresson - Lock at Bougival, France, 1955
(5) Stain glass windows at Sainte-Chapelle, Paris XIV century
(6) Église Notre-Dame-de-la-Nativité de Malay - Romanesque architecture church in Burgundy, France
(7) Le Baiser de Auguste Rodin - Tuileries Gardens, Paris

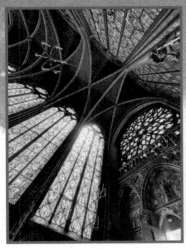

Reflective practice

1. Journal

"It's not always easy, I'll grant you that. It might even trigger the wounded child within you, and bring up traumas that you'd forgotten or didn't even know existed. And it is also your opportunity to become aware so you may clear and heal those wounds. You have a brand new, pure and loving heart in front of you, let them guide you and leave the rest behind." **Jeanne-Marie Paynel (2021)**

With this in mind, journal upon the following question:

*   What has your child taught you about yourself that you didn't already know?

2. Embodiment

When triggered by an event, a person, or a behaviour from our child, we should lovingly turn towards ourselves before and above everything else. We need to ensure that our inner child feels seen and heard first.

*   Place both hands on your heart, belly or any place on your body that feels most comforting and soothing. As you do so, say out loud, "Beloved, I see you, I am here for you." Allow yourself to feel soothed, allow yourself to feel seen, and repeat as often as needed.

Receiving self-compassion raises our resilience and allows us to offer compassion and empathy to others. This practice has been transformative for me on my healing journey. The words, as used above, first came to me from Christine of @the_ordinary_ sacred on Instagram.[3]

3. Creativity

"Education, as a whole, needs to be completely revamped. We're still operating with a 19th- century model, except we're now in the 21st century. Education as a whole needs to be taken apart and rebuilt so that our future generations are able to solve monumental issues" **Jeanne-Marie Paynel (2021)**

This is your space to create your version of an educational utopia using any method you wish, for example, journaling or drawing.

- If you could have the educational model that serves your deepest desires for humanity, what would that model look like?
- How do you see the future of education?
- What are the core values that you would establish?
- What would schools look like?
- How would they be run?
- What curriculum would be followed?
- Which communities would be served?
- What would the framework of education be at a governmental level?

Create and envision your aspirations for education that would serve future generations and a more peaceful humanity.

Share your thoughts...

I would love to hear your thoughts, so feel free to share them via any of the following ways to the Montessori Mission community:

- Email me sayhello@enrichingenvironments.com
- Tag me @enrichingenvironments and use the hashtag #montessorimission on Instagram & Facebook

CHAPTER 2

Akshatha Chandrakanth

Born in India and now living in Chicago, United States, on the original land of the Kiikaapoi people, Akshatha is a certified Positive Discipline Educator, AMI-trained Montessori Assistant for 0-3 and 3-6 years, and mother of a toddler.

With an infectious passion for Montessori, Akshatha is determined to adopt a positive and conscious parenting style which she shares, alongside her own parenting journey with her daughter, Maanvi, via her inspiring Instagram account, @maanvi_and_me. Akshatha also supports parents who are trying to intertwine their Indian culture with Montessori practices, and explores how they can work well together.

Akshatha:

Thank you so much for inviting me here today Charlotte. I am currently working on believing in myself, because I strongly feel that unless I believe in myself, it will be really hard for me to believe in my child. And when I saw the list of Montessorians you were going to interview, I really doubted myself, but then I had to stop and talk to myself; I may not be as experienced and I have never worked with children directly, but I do have a story I can share and love to share. And if it wasn't for Montessori, then I would never have had the guts to accept an invite like this. I have broken so many of my boundaries already, and it has been such a great transformation.

We begin the 10 Questions...

1. What does Montessori mean to you?

Akshatha:

Montessori has helped me in my spiritual journey, and that is one of the biggest reasons why I have a huge respect for Dr. Montessori's work. I truly believe that it is important for us to spiritually develop, so that we can meet the needs of our child. I really had to let go of many things, so much of my ego, my temper, my thinking; a whole mind shift had to happen.

My whole idea of what parenting is had to change in order to support my child and look at her as a free soul.

And the way I look at the world also had to change; if something goes wrong, let me see how I can solve it and move on. And this type of mindset comes naturally once we are on that path. Observation has helped me so much to get to know my child, as well as getting to know many things about myself, which I wasn't aware of before. Montessori has been such a beautiful thing that has happened in my life.

Charlotte:

It feels like a transformation for you in the way that you look at the world and that is so powerful. I can remember on my first day of training at Montessori Centre International in London, our lecturer said to us, "Once you start this course, you will never look at children in the same way again." And that really stuck with me.

2. What was your first light bulb moment on your Montessori journey?

Akshatha:

There have been many light bulb moments , but the first one was when I found out about Montessori. I was pregnant and working as a software developer in the United States , and I had started looking for day-care options. My company had just three months maternity leave, so I had to find a place from when my child was only 12 weeks old. I Googled and found Guidepost Montessori [1], which was only a block away from my house; they had a space for my newborn daughter in their Nido (a Montessori Infant Community for babies from approximately 12 weeks to walking), and I didn't even know what a Nido was! In this Nido I saw that they mentioned brain development, language development, hand development, independence and gaining more confidence in the eight weeks to 16 months' time frame. I was looking for a place where my child would be fed well, her hygiene would be taken care of, and where she felt secure, and I was very suspicious because it doesn't come naturally to think of independence and confidence with a newborn infant. That is when I started learning more, I looked at the classrooms and was so amazed to see that the children were so independent and doing things for themselves—it felt magical. Then when she was five months old, I found out that you don't need to be a trained Montessori Guide to practice Montessori at home. I learned that Montessori is a mindset of allowing our children the freedom to follow their own natural path of development. I figured out that they are capable, and that our role as parents is to guide them. We just have to give them an environment that is suited to their needs, and as much time and space as possible for them to follow their path and they can do it.

3. In what ways does Montessori enrich the work that you do?

Akshatha:

I don't work with children directly, but I do influence families through my work and my page. I see a lot of parents trying to get on board and practice Montessori, and I am really hoping that, if I am not influencing the children directly, I am helping them to take the Montessori path and live their life in a Montessori way. Of course, it has definitely helped me, as a parent, in my Montessori journey with my child. It fascinates me because, as Dr. Maria Montessori says, when we really give them that space and support, they really reveal themselves. Just my daughter Maanvi's body gestures, and the way she moves with confidence, and the way she does things is so magical, especially for a person like me, who has never seen a child do such things. So, it is definitely an amazing journey for me and I am looking forward to helping more children to come on this path.

Charlotte:

You are so right, magical is the word, when we can create the conditions, then the child does reveal his or herself.

Akshatha:

I feel so bad for little children who are seen as helpless, when it is adults who make them dependent, because they don't get an opportunity to practice the skills to become independent. I agree that it does take a lot of patience, and we have to slow down, and it does require a mind shift, but the smile on their face when they can accomplish something on their own is worth all of the effort we put in. That confidence and independence is what is so enriching for me about Montessori.

The Montessori Mission, by Charlotte Awdry

Charlotte:

The child is giving us the gift of understanding them deeper if we pay attention and, as you said, when they accomplish something, it comes from so deep within their heart; that is the magic.

Akshatha:

And that smile is what always stops me from interrupting her work. Especially when she is struggling; some say that it is the hardest moment for the child, but I think it is always the hardest for a parent to see their child struggle. Afterwards comes that smile of accomplishment and I don't want to steal that smile away from her.

Charlotte:

That is a lovely way of putting it. It is allowing us to just witness that and be part of that without needing to take over.

4. When was the first time a child taught you something about yourself that you weren't aware of?

Akshatha:

Right from the beginning when I had a two-day long labour. It was so memorable, it took almost three and a half to four hours just to push her out. Now when I think about it, it's like, how did I do that? I wanted it to be as natural as possible; it was painful, but it was an amazing journey, and it taught me a lot of lessons about myself.

Charlotte:

She is teaching you right from the beginning.

Akshatha:

Yes, my courage and my power; I don't know where that power comes from.

Charlotte:

It is ancient strength and wisdom, that sacredness of creation that gives us that strength when we need it; it is incredible and extraordinary.

5. When was the last time a child taught you something about yourself that you weren't aware of?

Akshatha:

I always say my child is my teacher, she teaches me every single day.

Currently my focus is on being in the moment, she says what she observes and it is amazing. She can point out a single dot, like an aeroplane in the far distance, or even an ant; she is so in tune with the surroundings.

And she tries to recognise all of the sounds, she wants to know what each sound is, which is really challenging for me because we live in downtown Chicago, and there are so many sounds! So, I am really trying to be more present and observant than I was before.

Charlotte:
There is something so magical, sharing the joy in the wonder of the world through their eyes, particularly for the Toddler age where Maanvi is at the moment. As you say, they teach us to be present and they teach us to observe because they are such keen, sharp observers.

Akshatha:
I try to be in the present because there is constantly something she is observing and I am observing her. It is magical and a different experience to see the world from her eyes.

Charlotte:
Giving them the gift of time and space is all we need to give them.

Akshatha:
It's not just for them, it is so good for us too.

6. When was the last time a child caught you out of integrity and questioned you on it?

Akshatha:
I have never shared this very personal story before, but it has really taught me some great lessons. Last December I lost my dad; it was a very emotionally draining moment for me and I decided that I would not cry or show my emotions to my daughter. I would do it differently now, but back then I was still in the learning phase, so I was trying to be as normal as possible. In fact, I was actually trying to be more active with her, and spending more time with her than usual just to cover it up. But then one night she didn't sleep, it was crazy, she was screaming, and I didn't know what was happening. I tried co-sleeping with her but it didn't help at all. Finally, I asked my husband to come and sleep with us, he brought his mattress and then I relaxed, and she relaxed too and fell asleep. I started analysing what had happened. I knew she

was very sensitive to order, and I was checking to see if anything had changed, but there was nothing. It was then that I realised it was me, that my emotional bucket was empty. I was trying to act normal, but she was so in tune with me that she noticed that something was wrong and was not comfortable with it. It struck me that it was not going to work if I tried to act in a certain way, and that I really needed to work on myself to change internally. What I say should come from my heart and, whatever I say, I have to mean it. This is the only way it is going to work, otherwise she won't connect with it because it's not coming from my heart. So, that was a really big transformation for me.

From then on, I have taken my internal journey, my spiritual journey very seriously and have started working on myself.

Whenever I feel like I have said something that did not come from my heart, I revisit those scenarios and ask myself, "What happened there? Why wasn't it coming from my heart?"

Charlotte:

That is such a beautiful and vulnerable story to share, thank you so much. They just sense our inauthenticity 50 miles away. If we are not aligned in some way, they know that something isn't right, they feel it. This is why we talk so much about the spiritual nature of the child and the child coming to us to teach us and reveal themselves. Maanvi knew that something was wrong with you and that was very confusing for her, with her ancient wisdom she sensed that. It is so humbling that a toddler can teach us a lesson of integrity, that is really powerful. As you say, it is part of our journey and it needs to be this way if we are going to create a new world. And if we are going to create a more peaceful and harmonious society, we need our children to be able to call us out and question our integrity. Because if they don't feel safe enough to do that, how can they feel safe enough in the world to question injustice? And how can they feel safe enough to question inequality and stand up for what is right if they can't call us out in an authentic way?

Akshatha:

I am so glad they do it because when they call us out it is a way for us to grow internally to greatness.

7. How did you explain yourself to your child afterwards?

Akshatha:

It was a big change for me. As soon as I relaxed, I just cried the whole night, and I was really relaxed the next day. I have had to rethink many things, and whatever I say to her has to come from my heart. It is still a work in progress, but I have improved a lot over the last few months of my journey.

8. What is your favourite Dr. Montessori quote?

Akshatha:

The one that I picked for today is, "A child without a secret becomes an adult without personality."[2] It's from *Dr Montessoris Speaks to Parents*. For a long time, I wanted to know what Maanvi was doing and thinking, I just wanted to get into her mindset. I think that as they grow up and go out into the world, the curiosity to know what is going on in their life might increase, and sometimes it is hard to just let go, but it is okay for them to have a secret. Of course, we had secrets that we didn't share with our parents, so it's not fair for us to watch everything that a child is doing. That's life isn't it? As long as they feel safe enough to come and talk to us if they want anything, that is all we can ask for.

Charlotte:

It is like when we learn to observe, as you said earlier on, being in that present moment and just honouring and revering what they are experiencing in that moment without us going 10 minutes ahead and working out what they are doing and the reasons for it. It is bringing ourselves back, really gently, and trying to make out what they are doing right now, instead of racing ahead.

9. What is your deepest desire for Montessori in the future?

Akshatha:

I have two. I want education in this school to be more accessible and affordable at the same time, because I hear people say: "I want my child to go to a Montessori school but I don't have a Montessori school where I live." Even if it is there, it is usually for the three to six age group, and after this age group there is no Montessori school available. And they get worried about their transition to a regular school after they have been to a Montessori school for so long. So, I really hope it becomes more accessible with more and more Montessori schools. And as Jeanne-Marie Paynel mentioned, if the education system follows the Montessori system, that would be awesome. But I hope there will be more Montessori schools that are affordable. I don't know about other parts of the world, but where I live it's super-expensive, and there are very few public Montessori schools. The next one is the community. I would like more families to actually start following Montessori with their children and in the right way. I am saying

The Montessori Mission, by Charlotte Awdry

the right way, because I am so happy to see the community growing, especially on social media.

I feel there is so much hype given to the shelf activities and the setup that we lose the core concepts and principles with time.

I don't know how much of the principle is actually being applied when I see some shelf setups that have all the expensive toys, and the child is always being corrected on how to do it. So, I really hope it spreads in the right way, and more people feel that they can actually follow Montessori principles with their children—that is my dream.

Charlotte:

Montessori is a way of life; we can practice it whether or not we have toys or other equipment or materials. It is a way of being with our child but also being with ourselves; understanding who we really are, what our passion is, what guides us, what our prejudices are, the way we limit ourselves and our children. That is what Montessori means to me.

10. What do you see is your role in achieving this desire?

Akshatha:

I am trying to help families, and show a small community the beauty of the Montessori home. I used to share the shelf activities, but I started getting a lot of questions about it and I felt like I was creating a disconnection with other parents which I really didn't want to do. That is when I started shifting my focus on my page away from the shelf, and more on giving value to the principles and showing practical life activities. Now I see more parents getting on board and showing more interest, sharing things that they have observed, and this is exactly what I want to convey to the world.

Charlotte:

That is such vital work, to move it away from purely aesthetics and focus more on the child and their needs. I think that is a metaphor for social media and life in general. It feels like more and more people in the world are more focused on aesthetics and the way that we look or the way that our homes look, and actually when we are able to and when it is the right time in our development or stage of our life, then we can come back to really what is inside. Our children really shine a light on this and, as you said, you realised that from the questions they were giving you that it wasn't really a reflection of what was in your heart, and how your heart wanted to speak about Montessori. So, that has guided you towards a different path and I think that is so valuable to the families that you work with.

MAITHREEM BHAJATHA
BY H.H CHANDRASEKARA SARASWATHI

ENGLISH REPRESENTATION OF SANSKRIT

maitrīṃ bhajata akhilahṛjjetrīm

ātmavadeva parānapi paśyata |

yuddhaṃ tyajata spardhāṃ tyajata

tyajata pareṣu akramam ākramaṇam ||

jananī pṛthivī kāmadughā(ā)ste

janako devaḥ sakaladayāluḥ |

dāmyata datta dayadhvaṃ janatāḥ

śreyo bhūyāt sakalajanānām ||

Maithreem Bhajatha Akila Hrith Jeththreem –Serve with Friendship and Humility, which will conquer the Hearts of Everyone.

Atmavat Eva Paraan Api Pashyata – Look upon others similar to yourself.

Yuddham Tyajata – Renounce War

Spardhaam Tyajata – Renounce unnecessary Competition for Power

Tyajata Pareshwa Akrama Aakramanam – Give up Aggression on others' properties which is wrong

Jananee Prithivee Kaamadughaastey – Mother Earth is wide enough and ready to give us all we desire like a Kaamadenu(Divine cow who can provide whatever one desires)

Janako Deva: Sakala Dayaalu: – God, Our Father, is very Compassionate to All

Daamyata – So, Restrain yourself

Datta – So, Donate your wealth to others

Dayathvam – So, Be Kind to others

Janathaa: – Oh People of the World

Shreyo Bhooyaath Sakala Janaanaam –May All People of this World be Happy and Prosperous.

Shreyo Bhooyaath Sakala Janaanaam – May All People of this World be Happy and Prosperous.

Shreyo Bhooyaath Sakala Janaanaam – May All People of this World be Happy and Prosperous.

Rangoli – is something very commonly found in hindu households. Some prefer to do it every single day. Every morning even before breakfast they clean the house entrance and draw these beautiful designs in front of the house. It's usually done with powdered limestone or dry rice flour. I remember doing it at my grandma's place and it used to feel so good to start our day by pouring out the creativity in us.

It not only starts our day well but also makes home feel so welcoming. This practice also has many benefits for our health and our home.

Bharatanatyam – There are 8 different classical dance forms of India. And Bharatanatyam is famous in the region I belong to and so it is very dear to my heart. I find it very expressive and people do several years of sadhana (practice) to master the art of Bharatanatyam.

Veena – India has a wide variety of musical instruments. It is really hard to count the varieties we have. Among them Veena and flute are my favorite. I find it so relaxing and meditative to listen to the carnatic music in these instruments.

Temples - India is known for its spirituality and religious diversity. and is filled with Hindu temples, mosques, churches etc. I belong to the southern part of India from a place called Dakshina Kannada which is very well known for its temples. Temples are not just buildings but a really beautiful art form and they are built keeping a lot of scientific and spiritual reasons in mind. The sculptures in Indian temples tell a lot of stories and show the richness in our culture. The picture below is one of the temples in my city in India.

Seemantham (Baby shower ceremony) - I celebrated my pregnancy with Seemantham. The plate full of food served, the fertile areca flower on my head, two kids sitting beside me, everything has a significance in the ritual.

Mehendi (henna art) - Mehendi designs are a part of our major celebrations. A Hindu bride looks incomplete without henna in her hands and henna is considered very auspicious in our celebrations. The day before the wedding is dedicated to the mehendi function and it is given almost the same importance as a wedding. The picture here was taken before my seemantham. The ceremony happens almost as grand as the wedding so we do apply mehendi on our hands before the seemantham.

Krisha Vesha (Krishna Costume) - Krishnashtami is a Hindu festival celebrated throughout the country to welcome Lord Krishna home and celebrate his birth. We dress up our little ones like Lord Krishna. This is Maanvi in Krishna costume.

Reflective practice

1. Journal

"I truly believe that it is important for us to spiritually develop, so that we can meet the needs of our child. I really had to let go of many things, so much of my ego, my temper, my thinking; a whole mind shift had to happen. My whole idea of what parenting is had to change in order to support my child and look at her as a free soul."
Aksthatha Chandrakanth (2021)

Akshatha speaks of how she needed to change in order to support her daughter and meet her needs. With this in mind, journal upon the following thoughts:

- In what ways have you developed and grown since becoming a parent, educator or caregiver?
- Did you have any previous perceptions or opinions about children before you became a parent, educator or caregiver? If so, what were they? How have they been challenged since?
- Have you experienced a significant light bulb moment in one particular area?

2. Embodiment

"The smile on their face when they can accomplish something on their own is worth all of the effort we put in." **Aksthatha Chandrakanth (2021)**

- The next time your child achieves or completes something for themselves, observe their reaction without responding or praising. Try to be with them in that moment as part of their joy without needing to add anything to it.
- How does it feel in your body to be part of their magical moments of accomplishment?

3. Creativity

"I try to be in the present because there is constantly something she is observing and I am observing her. It is magical and a different experience to see the world from her eyes."
Aksthatha Chandrakanth (2021)

- The next time you are with a toddler, observe them exploring their world. Notice their interest in the world around them, and how they are experiencing life through all of their senses.
- Bring this same quality of attention to your next experience in nature. What can you hear, close by and in the distance? What can you smell? What textures can you feel? As an example, this could be the different types of bark on trees.
- Hugging trees is a beautiful daily practice for children and adults alike. Wrap your arms around a tree to experience the full body sensation of being grounded into the earth.

Becoming aware of specific senses when we are outdoors, and appreciating nature's gifts connects us to our creativity and inner peace. Notice how you and your child feel and behave after intentional moments outdoors.

Share your thoughts...

I would love to hear your thoughts, so feel free to share them via any of the following ways to the Montessori Mission community:

- Email me sayhello@enrichingenvironments.com
- Tag me @enrichingenvironments and use the hashtag #montessorimission on Instagram & Facebook

Nusaibah Macadam

Born and raised in the UK, and now living in Malaysia since 2016, Nusaibah is the Principal of Rumi Montessori; the school is a stalwart in the Montessori community and seeks to be a pioneer in Islamic education in Malaysia.

Nusaibah has a Casa classroom (Age 3-6 years) and an Elementary classroom (Age 6 - 12 years). She is a Montessori teacher, trainer and consultant, and is the founder of the first Islamic Montessori magazine.

Nusaibah's son, Noah, is a Montessori child from birth and is homeschooling himself at the age of 17. And it is so interesting following Nusaibah and her son's journey on Instagram @rumi_montessori through the videos and stories she posts.

Coincidentally, Nusaibah is also a friend of the principal of Mon Ecole in Dubai, the Montessori school that my children, Olivia and Harry attend. So, it's a really, really small world.

We begin the 10 Questions...

1. What does Montessori mean to you?

Nusaibah:

This is an answer that evolves over time. In every stage of my life, Montessori has meant something different and it is still evolving and growing. But what's really coming to me during this particular time period is everybody finding their unique purpose in this cosmos, whether it's for the child, for you as a Montessori guide, for a teacher, or a parent. Montessori is discovering your place in the cosmos and in this universe. What is your place and what is your purpose and what are you going to do? In Montessori, you have stages of development, and in each one of those stages the child is seeking to create their character and their personality, and discover their place in this universe. And so, what really comes to me all the time is that Montessori is this journey of self-discovery. You are discovering yourself, discovering your universe, discovering your purpose and realising who you are, and what you are here for, and for every person it is unique. Everyone comes with a unique perspective and gift to discover, and that discovery starts from birth. Montessori is aiding that journey, so that each individual can find out who they truly are, and become their true authentic selves. That's the one that's really sitting with me right now. As I go deeper and deeper, it's not just the child that's transformed by Montessori, but adults are also transformed, whether you are a formally trained Montessori guide, or you are a parent who is just finding out about Montessori, or even if you don't have your own children. When you learn about the Montessori philosophy in theory, you become transformed and you become a better version of yourself. It shows you that this journey of self-discovery is applicable to the child, it's applicable to the adult, it's applicable across the board. And I think that is what Montessori really brings to our lives and that is what it means for me right now. However you touch this Montessori world, it transforms you in some way or another and that's the beautiful thing. Having a 17-year-old, and seeing him from birth all the way, he's in that third plane of development, he's not done yet with his discovery. It's not necessarily a journey of academics or a journey of learning. but it is a journey of discovering who he is in this universe, in this cosmos. It is very beautiful to watch and very beautiful to be part of.

2. What was your first light bulb moment on your Montessori journey?

Nusaibah:

The early part of my schooling was in a Montessori school and I remember feeling harmony and tranquillity—there was nothing against me, no pressure or force pushing me off my path. In Montessori we believe the child is guided from within, they have that inner teacher that is guiding them, and I was very much in touch with my inner teacher. Unfortunately, I had to leave the Montessori setting later on in my Elementary years.

When I went into a mainstream setting, even though my parents tried to choose a really good private mainstream school, that experience was so evident to me as a child that this is not who I am, and this is not what I am doing, this is not what I know or do not know. I remember as a child coming out from that Montessori environment and going into a mainstream environment and thinking: "What on the earth are these people doing? What is the point of this? How come they don't know who I am?" That experience of transitioning from Montessori to mainstream had already brought up something inside me, and I carried that throughout the rest of my schooling years. Some people hear that story and they say, "I must never put my child in mainstream school after Montessori," or, "I do not want my child to go through that, so I won't put them in Montessori from the start." I'm not saying it is a negative experience, in fact that experience has been so powerful for me because it's helped me to create who I am now, it has helped me to have that awareness of education, of people, of supporting development. It raised this awareness in me: "What is the purpose of being a child?" I was a child, and I was thinking, "Why am I a child? What are we supposed to be doing? Why do these adults just not understand us? Why do they have to make us do something or make us be in some way?" That questioning was with me, and it was really strong. And when I was 16, 17 years old, there was a really strong force inside me saying, "This cannot be right. This way of education, this way of talking to children, it's not fruitful, it's not letting people discover who they are. It's breaking people or shaping people into a mould."

Montessori tells us that the adolescent is searching for their identity, and they have this really strong sensitivity to justice, and to social systems. I was going through that as a teenager, but I was not in a Montessori setting, I did not have a Montessori home. My parents did put me in a Montessori school but they were not doing Montessori at home, I did not have that at home like so many children luckily have today. But that questioning was there because that is a natural part of development. And because I had that previous Montessori experience, I was in touch with my inner teacher, so I could see those questions coming. And then watching people grow around me, my friends, my siblings and seeing these wonderful, amazing, bright, curious young children who grew alongside me who had no interest or capability to teach themselves, no drive. I remember seeing that as a teenager and thinking, "That's not right. I need to train as a Montessori teacher because we need to make sure that this history is not repeating itself over and over again."

The Montessori Mission, by Charlotte Awdry

I actually started my Montessori training when I was 17. I had to put in a special request to join the course because I was really young. I was interviewed by Barbara Isaacs who was at Montessori Centre International at that time, and she heard my story and let me come on board the course. That's how my journey continued in Montessori. I really believe the light bulb comes on when you are a child in the Montessori environment, and it changes something inside you. And that has really been a huge force directing me to where I have come, what I have understood, and all the work that I have tried to do. That first experience of realising the difference between the harmonious development, according to the natural human stages, and the natural human rhythm, and then seeing the extreme between that and this other system, which is not based on how humans are, or how humans grow, or how humans develop. It is based on a system that is wanting to create something specific or guide something specific. Whereas in Montessori, you are going with that natural rhythm and the end result is that unique individual and personality.

3. In what ways does Montessori enrich the work that you do?

Nusaibah:

Montessori allowed me to discover who I am.

> *In order for you to do something effectively and beautifully, you really need to be in touch with who you are. You need to be able to recognise your strengths and your weaknesses, your whole package, so that you can be your authentic self.*

Montessori has allowed me to understand myself and make the most of who I am. Montessori helps you to bring out a strength inside you that is in you already. It has allowed me to understand myself, and through understanding myself it has given me that vision of finding my purpose and led me to Montessori training. If I didn't have Montessori education, I may have gone into child psychology. But the beautiful thing about Montessori is you don't just understand the human being, you understand yourself and the context of humans within this cosmos. It's really enriched that, and allowed me, in my work, to really focus on what it is that I love, which is to see that potentiality in the human being, whether it is a child, or whether it is a lady who is working with me in school, or a family. I love seeing that potentiality in the individual, and then facilitating it by removing obstacles and creating an environment that allows people to grow. On a bigger scale, Montessori is allowing us to discover our potential realities and the potentialities of those around us, and then creating that environment where everybody can flourish, so that each person's uniqueness can shine. That is humanity.

Charlotte:

So beautiful and so true. As you said earlier on, allowing the uniqueness of each child to come forth, we are not trying to put a square peg into a round hole, everyone gets to give their gifts. In the film, Inside Montessori (Quiet Island Films, 2019), one of the Elementary guides says that the beauty about Elementary Montessori is that each child realises that they have a gift to give that is unique, that nobody else has. And this speaks to what you're saying.

4. When was the first time a child taught you something about yourself that you weren't aware of?

Nusaibah:

When I first went into a Montessori classroom as an adult and saw how the children worked without the need of an adult, how they worked independently, and the amazing things that they could do. It really gave me that realisation: I am not here to be your teacher because you, child, are capable of so much. I'm not here to teach you and give you my knowledge, you're here to teach me to grow and to show me this capability, this immense potentiality that is within you. We are on this journey together, there is no hierarchy of, I'm the adult, you are the child; I'm giving, you are taking. This is a mutual journey where there is learning coming from both, and a growth in both. That was the first thing, observing the classroom and seeing the children in action, and realising I was powerless, and that I had to take a step back from the idea that is programmed into us from a young age, that we are the adults and therefore "we know!" We have to clear that out from us and once we clear it out, we see the magic happen. If you go to a mainstream classroom it is the complete opposite because the adult is in control. That adult is the one who is leading, and the child has their attention and is doing what that adult has asked them, so it is very adult-centred. Whereas in the Montessori environment, the adult is not there, so we can see who the child is. They show us that they are truly capable of developing and creating themselves in the most beautiful ways possible. So that really struck me.

Charlotte:

Amazing. There is a Dr. Montessori quote when she talks about the spiritual preparation of the adult where she talks about tearing out the roots of our prejudice, I remember reading that in my training and it really stuck with me. As you say, whether it is a classroom setting or in the home, that is what our children invite us to do every single day. There isn't a cardboard cut-out solution we can provide; our child is there in front of us and we must answer the soul of the child, we cannot just put these predetermined parameters of control on them.

5. When was the last time a child taught you something about yourself that you weren't aware of?

Nusaibah:

I came to Malaysia as a foreigner, not knowing the language, not knowing the culture, not knowing the way things are. I came to a very new environment and I remember feeling nervous and worried about opening up my school and having these children who speak another language. I look different, I sound different, everything is different. I remember those first few days...

> *That boundless love of the child, they don't discriminate, by nature they accept everybody, the beautiful things and the flaws.*

I really experienced that from the root when I first opened my Montessori school because it is a completely different culture. Seeing these children accept me for how I am and with that love, and then that journey of observing these children, how they will accept anybody, that boundless love that is the inner child, has really touched me and taught me that this is what it means to be human. And if we don't have that within us, and sadly we see so much on the news and on social media today, we are bombarded by this discrimination. But when you look at the child, they do not live like that, and they do not act like that, they do not see like that. Experiencing them with every new person that comes to the environment, every new face, every person, culture, children with disabilities, seeing how they truly accept them wholeheartedly, has really taught me that we need to change ourselves inside, so that we have that same boundless love that we can offer to everybody.

> *Because when you look at the child, what you see is the true meaning of humanity.*

That united humanity that Montessori talks about, you see that in the child. And if we see them, and we look at ourselves, we can see what we need to change in ourselves, so that we can become a true human, in that sense of boundless love and acceptance for all.

Charlotte:

As you said, the child has that boundless love and expansiveness within them, and as parents and guides, how do we honour that? How do we revere that? What can we do as parents and as guides to make sure that that light does not go out? How can we support our child in the best way, so that what is inside of them is honoured, appreciated, nourished, nurtured and grown rather than dimmed by quite an unrelenting world at times?

Nusaibah:

I think this is a really interesting question that I keep reflecting on myself. How can we keep that alive in the child? Especially in this time that we are living in, where there is so much noise in the background. One aspect is that we give them a variety of experiences, to make sure there is diversity, but that is a very surface level aspect. I've been reading more about Dr. Montessori, her work, especially in her book, Education and Peace (Dr Maria Montessori, 1949). She really emphasises that if the child is able to develop according to nature, they will not come off that track because it is innate within the child. They only stop being like that when we take them off track.

It is about allowing the child to develop according to the plan of nature because when the child develops according to the plan of nature, they will be love.

Dr Montessori said: "Two paths lie open in the development of personality – one that leads to the man who loves and one that leads to the man who possesses. One leads to the man who has won his independence and works harmoniously with others, and the other to the human slave who becomes the prisoner of his possession as he tries to free himself and who comes to hate his fellows. These two paths might be called the paths of good and of evil, one leads to heaven and the other to hell, one leads man to his supernatural perfection, and the other takes him below his own natural level."[1] This oppression that we see around us, each person who oppresses has been oppressed, but when does oppression start? The first oppression we experience as a child when we want to follow our natural path of development, we want to follow our natural inner drive, but we are prevented, that's oppression. We are oppressing the child and creating an imbalance in the harmony of their development. And when we create this imbalance, it leads to their personality developing in a way that does not have that full love and respect and harmony with the universe around them. If we really come back to allowing the child to develop according to the plan of nature, so that they can become who they are in harmony with that environment, that love will shine through, that love will be there. If we can allow that development to happen, according to nature and how it should be, that is one huge step to saving the child from developing a personality that is not in harmony.

Charlotte:

It is a huge responsibility. As Dr. Montessori said: the child is born innately good. We have to hold that in our minds and in our hearts all of the time, even if they are doing something which is undesirable or destructive. We have to hold the image in our minds that the child is innately good. And a problem I see within Western society is the notion that the child is not good, so we need to discipline them to make them good; but that is all back to front isn't it?

Discipline is about connection; it is not about control. This is rewiring everything and now there is this collective consciousness that is rising about it.

There are more and more resources available to people on social media and online, but it is so amazing that Dr. Montessori was talking about this long before anyone else was talking about collective consciousness. She was on it before any of us even knew what it was, which is really extraordinary.

Nusaibah:

When they say Montessori is timeless, it truly is because 100 years later it is still as relevant as it was.

Charlotte:

Even more relevant. There are more people on the planet, bigger challenges, more discord, more disharmony. As you said a few moments ago, there is more noise.

6. When was the last time that a child caught you out of integrity and questioned you on it?

Nusaibah:

In my work, we have a 3-6 year old environment, an Elementary environment and I actually live in an Adolescents' community. What has been really interesting is seeing in each plane of development how the child will show you what you need to change about yourself. So, in the three to six environment, if you come in with the wrong energy, or you are coming in out of integrity, you are immediately going to see that the child acts differently, you are going to see it in how they act. When you come to the Elementary stage, if you do something that is out of integrity, they will just tell you, they will say, "That is not fair, that was not kind," or, "You did not respect me." But when it comes to the adolescent stage. This is hugely interesting for me. My latest experience is with my own son who is 17 and in adolescence.

Adolescents are really sensitive to social justice, not just to themselves or to their friends or to their family, but they are really interested in global justice, they are concerned about all humans. It is a very deep, unified way that they are interested in injustice.

Noah has made me question my own ideas and prejudice that I hold on certain topics. He has made me question fairness; not the fairness that the Elementary child asks us, but is that really fair for humanity? Is it really fair when you think of somebody like that, or when you talk about somebody like that? Is that truly honouring the human being? Adolescents are searching so deep within themselves to discover who they are, especially those adolescents who have had a Montessori experience from birth. When you make a statement or when you hold a belief about something that is not in harmony with the universe, or in harmony with nature, they will hold you accountable and question you. And I am having this every day with my son right now at the age of 17, having to really dig deep into who I am and what beliefs, values and morals I hold.

Charlotte:

The best of who you want to be, the best of who you seek for yourself. I'm not there with teenagers yet, but Olivia is six and a half and in the past six months she has given me a really good wake-up call in terms of integrity, calling me out on things and questioning injustice in the world. It is powerful and we have got to have an answer to these things. What is so beautiful about doing this path and, particularly because I work a lot with toddlers, people think that this is going to make parenting easy, but it is actually going to make it harder because you are growing people, you are not growing robots. This is a human who is going to question you and challenge you and ask you and push you and test you. It is not about making a child better behaved, it is about, like you said, getting ready, preparing for what the child is going to show you about yourself.

Nusaibah:

They will question and they will explore and they want to come to their own independent conclusions, so they are not going to become that copy of who you want them to be. So, in one aspect it is harder if you are trying to do something to the child. But on another aspect, it's easier because they are so in touch with who they are. Montessori children, especially in the teenage years, are less likely to give in to peer pressure and do something that is wrong, just because everybody is pushing them to do it. So, that makes your life easier because you have a solid person there who is not going to do something dangerous or harmful to someone else. But I think in the end, the beautiful thing is, when you have your child...

Who do you want to actually meet? Do you want to meet the child that you moulded and you formed? Or do you want to actually get to know your real child? Do you want to get to know that real individual that is in your child?

That is a question that I always asked myself with Noah. Do I want Noah to become who I want him to be? Or do I really want to know who he is? When you allow them the space to be themselves, you see something so beautiful that you could not even imagine.

The Montessori Mission, by Charlotte Awdry

7. How did you explain yourself when you were out of integrity?

Nusaibah:

Noah will say to me, "Where did that belief come from? Where did you get it? How did you create that belief within yourself?" It could be something small, a belief that eating lots of fried food is unhealthy, but where did it come from? And what I have realised is that you have to explore that conversation together. First of all, I have to be ready to accept that I may be wrong, "Maybe frying food is not so bad, let's look at this together. You can do the research and you can give me the information." And, sometimes, I have to accept that I might have to change my mindset, I might have to change what I have believed all of these years.

Charlotte:

Humility is the word that comes to me in neon lights!

Nusaibah:

He went through this stage where he fell in love with butter. And I was saying, "No. You shouldn't eat too much butter, it's not good for your health." And he was like, "There are people who say that butter is good for you. When you buy the butter, I want the best butter and I will eat it all! Did you know that in the history of the world people ate a lot more butter than they eat now?" So, again, it may be something I have been programmed to believe, "Don't have too much butter, it's not good for you." But actually, maybe there is some truth, there are diets now where you have more butter and oils and it is supposed to be more healthy for you. When he holds me accountable for a principle or moral belief, then the conversation has to go to that exploration.

I have to be ready to be able to voice my opinion in a way that is respectful to another adult because these adolescents are new adults. But at the same time being ready that he might teach me something new. And if he teaches me something new, I should be happy to take it on.

These are small things that I'm talking about but they do it on the small and the large scale, and we need to be ready. Six months ago, he said to me, "You know what? I don't think I believe in the Montessori system." I was like, "WHAT?" He listed his reasons and then I told him why I really believe in it, but I had to be prepared, maybe there is something more he is showing me that I don't know. Anyway, in the conclusion, he said that every child should have a Montessori education and every adult should learn about Montessori because it helps them to get in touch with who they are and what the purpose of their life is. In the end, I didn't have to give up and now he has come on board Montessori even stronger. We might not have had that beautiful outcome if

I didn't allow him to hold me accountable and allow that conversation to happen. Of course, he has experienced Montessori first-hand through growing up and through me. But he's gone beyond that, he's looked online and sought out different things. There is division and hierarchy in Montessori, and I think when he saw that, through his own exploration, that's when he questioned, "Well, that's not humanity."

And this is truly the beauty of the adolescent, they teach us so much. They even hold us accountable to how true we are to the Montessori method, or how true we are to this vision that Dr. Montessori had. I talk about him a lot and share about him because I know that there are so many parents out there right now that have young children who are wondering if they are doing the right thing. How is their child going to be? What does this journey look like? When he was young, I had all those questions and I could not find the answers. So, I think it's lovely if more of us who have these Montessori teenagers share, so those who have younger children can know that it is okay, it is worth the journey. The Montessori child is in touch with themselves, they know who they are. Noah went to a Montessori school, he had the Montessori materials, he was in the Montessori environment. But actually, looking back at his childhood, the memories that stand out the most are those real-life experiences that he had, especially the ones in nature. Those are the ones that stood out the most to him and those are the ones that have empowered him to become who he is today. For us going to the park was a daily part of our life; instead of driving to school, we cycled to school, and I would plan the route through the park, so every day he got to have this real-life experience in nature—it was part of his life. I think that we really need to look at our lives and look at how we can make nature part of our everyday life, but it is not limited to the park. Bring plants into your home, make a little balcony or if you don't have a balcony, make window plants and bring nature inside.

You can observe the roots growing from an onion, whatever it may be, you can collect seeds from your fruit, you can have little creepy crawlies, my house was full of creepy crawlies when he was younger. Just let the child live with nature.

I believe that they need to see us fall in love with nature. So, for those who are not in touch with nature, buy a plant and fall in love with that plant, and let the child see you pay attention to that plant. Talk to your plants, water your plant with care, with love, let them see that connection.

And that is what they need to see to put them in touch with nature, especially if you are not somebody who is into animals or plants. My house is full of cats, we have always had these little other beings around us that require love and attention and it gives a beautiful experience for children. So, give that natural daily time to be with

The Montessori Mission, by Charlotte Awdry

nature, let it be part of life, not a scheduled time. Because nature is going to teach your children so much that you could never give to them in another way.

8. What is your favourite Dr. Montessori quote of today?

Nusaibah:

I have got loads of favourite quotes, but let me read the one that I just read earlier because it was really interesting; she says: "It has been said that man's greatest delight is to possess things. No. Man's greatest delight is to use them, using them to perfect himself, and at the same time to improve his environment." Later on, she says, "This great revelation we owe to the child lies open in the development of personality, one that leads to the man who loves and one that leads to the man who possesses; one leads to the man who has won his independence and works harmoniously with others, and the other to the human slave who becomes the prisoner of his possessions as he tries to free himself, and who comes to hate his fellows." [2] She is making it so clear to us that every child has a path that is going to lead them to be in harmony with their environment, to be full of love and to reach their full potential. We need to just get out of the way, remove the obstacles and prepare the environment to aid that to happen. We are not making it happen, we are not guiding them to make it happen; we are letting it happen naturally by removing the obstacles and preparing the environment.

9. What is your deepest desire for Montessori in the future?

Nusaibah:

I would love Dr. Montessori's vision to become accessible to all children and adults. What really struck me when I first came to Malaysia is the commercialisation of Montessori. It's really hard to run a school in England and a lot of people who run Montessori schools or preschools are not making a profit from it. It is a passion, a labour of love for a lot of people in England because it is a very difficult thing to achieve. I would really love Montessori education to be accessible to all children, at all levels of society, especially those children who are special needs and who need it so much. I do not think there has been enough work to help parents to understand their children. This knowledge has been around for more than 100 years, but there are so many parents who still have no clue. I feel like there has not been enough work, of letting community, on a wider scale, understand the human being, understand the child, understand themselves, understand the gift that Montessori brings to the life of people. That is why I really love when I see people who start to work with parents, a Montessori Guide like yourself. It's not just about implementing Montessori in a school. If we really want to have that impact, it is about Montessori being accessible for all and that knowledge being accessible for all. I really hope that over the coming years we can reach a place where there is that mutual respect and understanding and collaboration, so that we can serve the child the way that they should be served, especially those who are coming from poverty or the millions of refugee children that we have in the world. I really hope that Montessori can become accessible to them.

Charlotte:
That is a beautiful vision, effecting massive social change.

Nusaibah:
That is what the child needs and that is what they deserve. If we can do that on a wider scale, people can begin to understand human development and the child. Hopefully this is going to bring that shift that we need for the future. That is what Dr. Montessori was trying to achieve, that is what she was trying to do. So, we need to also be the agents in that work and hopefully we can make a change.

Charlotte:
We can. That is the vision of the Montessori Mission, every Montessorian is from a different environment, setting and community perspective. My vision is to show that it is not just for the white European, it is for everyone in every home. So, people can see it is not just for the stereotypical pretty pictures on Instagram, there is a lot more breadth and depth to it that, as you said, can be offered to every child and should be offered to every child, no matter what circumstance they grow up in. That is our work.

Nusaibah:
That is definitely our work. And, hopefully, we live to see the change that takes place.

10. What do you see is your role in achieving this desire?

Nusaibah:
For now I am trying to do the work that I can in Malaysia, to make an impact here. I have been here for five years and it's been really beautiful to see the shift in parents who are now beginning to understand their children. In Malaysia, my focus is to try and get that beautiful wisdom and knowledge that Montessori has out there, but in a really approachable way and a way that is accessible for all. The Montessori philosophy, theory and understanding of the human being does not cost anything. I really love that there are these amazing courses available and I really recommend for people who can, to join courses, and there are amazing books to read. But at the same time, this knowledge can also be shared amongst people, so I'm trying to do my best

with that. Working together with other Montessorians and other like-minded people is really what we need to be doing, and I hope that I can be of service to this, so that this knowledge of Montessori is accessible and is given in a way that is easy to understand. In the end, it is not about the adult who is going to hear this and make a change in their house, or the course that we ran, everything is about the child who is going to be on the receiving end. And, for me, happiness comes from knowing that there are children in their homes having that experience where they can be themselves and develop according to nature.

Charlotte:

As you said, we get out of the way and we just focus on the child and the child's needs and where they are. She said, follow the child, she gave us some very simple instructions, you don't need to do anything else.

Nusaibah:

It is really straightforward and simple but we find it difficult, we have to start to reprogram our mind, our language, our thought process, everything. Once you do that reprogramming it becomes your nature, because that is your nature.

As human beings, we come back to our nature. a better version of themselves. Who doesn't want to become a better version? Not only do you help the child, but you are helping yourself.

Charlotte:

And when we help ourselves, it has a ripple effect in our families and our communities. As you say, every time we come back to our true self, to our true nature, to our connection to source, however it resonates most to us, according to our belief system, it is a positive benefit to a more peaceful and harmonious world. And that is the gift that we can give our children, but we give ourselves also because it has this huge impact.

Nusaibah:

It is the gift that they were born with. And we have to try and make sure that they are not robbed of those gifts.

Nusaibah's chosen poem:.

RUMI

In your light I learn how to love.
In your beauty, how to make poems.
You dance inside my chest
where no-one sees you,
but sometimes I do,
and that sight becomes this art.

Nusaibah:: My life is infused with Rumi,
hence the name of my school!

Images: From top, left to right
(1) *Elementary children praying*
(2) *St.Michael's church in London where Nusaibah attended Montessori as a child*
(3) *Drumming*
(4) *Working with the division board*
(5) *Working with the moveable alphabet in Arabic*
(6) *Cat in the class!*
(7) *Noah following his interest in worms*
(8) *Nusaibah's own wood work*
(9) *Nusaibah's geometric designs*
(10) *Noah & Ustaz Soffhan in Sufi clothing*

A peek into the world of Nusaibah

Reflective practice

1. Journal

When I asked Nusaibah to describe her first light bulb moment on her Montessori journey, she identified the time when she moved into the Elementary stage of her education. She recalled deep questions arising within herself about what it was to be a child, and what she was meant to be doing during childhood.

With this in mind, in your journal, consider the following question:

- What is the purpose of being a child?

2. Embodiment

During our interview, Nusaibah describes how her son, Noah, has at times questioned her beliefs and her work. She explains how that has required her to be willing to examine her own values and beliefs, without feeling criticised or disrespected when he challenges her.

- What do you feel in your body when you perceive that your child is being rude, defiant, or questions your authority?
- Where are these sensations located? What is their colour and texture?
- In what ways can you conduct love through your body towards your child when there is a power struggle?

Perhaps you could envision light spreading from your body to theirs, or an invisible string connecting the two of you, both of you being wrapped up in a huge cuddle.

3. Creativity

'I really hope that over the coming years we can reach a place where there is that mutual respect and understanding and collaboration (within education), so that we can serve the child in the way that they should be served.' **Nusaibah Macadam (2021)**

- What would this vision of mutual respect, understanding and collaboration look like to you?

Write, draw, paint, dance, compose or sculpt your vision.

Share your thoughts...

I would love to hear your thoughts, so feel free to share them via any of the following ways to the Montessori Mission community:

- Email me sayhello@enrichingenvironments.com
- Tag me @enrichingenvironments and use the hashtag #montessorimission on Instagram & Facebook

CHAPTER 4

Trisha Moquino

Living on the lands of her people, the Kewa and Cochiti-Tribal Nations, Trisha Moquino is one of the founders of the Keres Children's Learning Centre (KCLC) in Cochiti Pueblo, New Mexico. The centre is an intergenerational Keres language revitalisation programme and is guided by Montessori pedagogy.

Trisha advocates for Indigenous communities to revitalise their languages, and has also been a powerful advocate for families reclaiming their children's education. One of her Instagram accounts is @indigenouscheerleader, which is just the perfect handle for her. She is a vital and hugely important force for anti-biased and anti-racist education. She was raised in a family who taught her a deep reverence, love and respect for her culture, traditions and language.

So, after graduating from Stanford University, she returned to New Mexico to help nurture the new generation of Keres-speaking people, children from Cochiti Pueblo, in her mission to raise up the importance of language and culture in order to maintain the tradition of the Keres-speaking Cochiti people and for Indigenous communities globally.

We begin the 10 Questions...

1. What does Montessori mean to you?

Trisha:

II first came across Montessori in 1999 when I was in my first year at the local public school, Cochiti Elementary, which is located on our reservation but is still very much an assimilationist model of education. In that first year I learned about Montessori from a woman at the school, called Ann Vallela, and as I started to understand a little bit more, I realised how it could help the tribe to revitalise our language. What spoke to me was her philosophy around cosmic education, especially at the Elementary age level. Her belief aligned with our belief, but our way of life has been around longer than the Montessori method—it has been around for thousands of years. Just as Dr Montessori says that every child has a cosmic purpose, our belief is the same.

We believe that every child is here for a reason, they have something to teach us, they all have gifts, and it is our job as adults to nurture those gifts. It is always to nurture those gifts in service to our people, in service to others and with love to others.

That has always really spoken to me. And so, in the creation of the KCLC, it is our language and culture, our values, our way of life that guides us, and we use Montessori in service to that mission. There is all this stuff coming up around boarding and residential schools in Canada. People are shocked but we know, it is in our lives, and is something that we have all learned to deal with. Monica Tsethlikai of Arizona State University (ASU) does a lot of research around how language and culture are protective factors. And we absolutely know that for those who did survive boarding school, that is probably what led them through. Back to what Montessori means to me: it is an opportunity to still provide children with the academic side of what they need to be as part of Western white culture, the dominant culture here in settler colonial United States, but not at the expense of losing us and losing our language. And that is what education has been on for far too long, so I am just really grateful for that.

Charlotte:

That is incredible how you saw those two things intertwined, as you say, the cosmic purpose and the purpose within the tribe of service to others. That is what Dr. Montessori wanted, the Elementary child to start becoming aware of their place in society and how they can give. And I love the way you said it, in service to others and in service to your people. And I guess in modern-day terms, if we are looking at conscious parenting, a lot of us want to raise our children as contributors rather than consumers, and it all intertwines. As you said, in your culture for thousands of years that has been ingrained, it has been part of the fabric of your culture, traditions, and your language, and how beautiful that Montessori has given a way to fit that together into the modern world.

2. What was your first light bulb moment on your own personal Montessori journey?

Trisha:

"It was a three-period lesson connection. In my first year teaching in 1999 at Cochiti Public School, I was immersed into learning about Montessori as they were trying to implement it there at the school. And I immediately remembered this idea of the 3 steps: - 1) this is 2) show me 3) tell me as I had already been introduced to it two years before working in our Tribe's Cochiti Summer Youth Language Program or CSYLP. Their language revitalisation program started in the summer of 1996 and I started teaching in it in the summer of 1997. The consultant that trained us in language revitalisation, Dr. Lily Wong Fillmore out of UC Berkeley (we call her, Chinese grandma), said that immersion is the way to go. She had two doctoral students under her, Rebecca Blum Martinez and Dr. Christine Sims, who is from the Keres-speaking Acoma Pueblo. They were the three people who guided us in this group and in the work, and they trained us really well in language immersion techniques during the summer of those first three years of training. They said immersion is the hardest, but it is the most effective, and it is what the native Hawaiians and Maori people use to revitalise their language. I was a younger person really blessed to be in the company of really fluent speakers and elders, many of whom have passed on, but we were all learning together about how to teach our language. I remember them teaching us that three-period lesson, Show me, Tell me. A year later, when I started my first year of teaching at the local public school, I was integrated into the K12 team and started learning about Montessori. When she talked about the three-period lesson, I was like, "Oh, I know what that is." Grandma Lily, Rebecca and Chris were not calling it the three-period lesson, but that was one of the major techniques, especially at the basic levels. Grandma Lily wasn't trained in Montessori, but she knew about it, had lots of experience and had worked with it, so I believe that is also where she learned that technique. For me, any lightbulb moment has always, first and foremost, been in the way that the philosophy aligns with our philosophy of children. Because the way that has been imposed on our people, as Indigenous peoples, and there are over 572 tribes that are still in existence today, has always been to centre English, and has tried, as General Pratt, the founder of the military boarding schools said, "Kill the Indian, save the man." With Montessori, I saw an opportunity for us to support our language and culture. Also, the way in which she recognises the spirit of the child and does not try to separate that, whereas in public school, there is that separation of state and church. Even though we are not a church, we are our own religion and way of life. And so, anything that I see that aligns with our philosophy around children is always a lightbulb moment and I continue to have those all the time.

Charlotte:

What I am hearing from you is that the spirit of the child is honoured first in Cochiti Pueblo. Any education, any input that we give as adults has to honour the child first and has to be harmonious. It's not just filling them with information, it has to be an enriching addition to the child, something that, as you say, can help them with a cosmic purpose, with how they are going to give their gifts to the world.

3. In what ways does Montessori enrich the work that you do?

Trisha:

One of the things I always remember Grandma Lily telling me is that, in some ways, because our people have been taught to be ashamed of who we are, we have been taught to be ashamed of our language, we have been taught to be ashamed of our culture, we have been taught that whiteness is something we should be trying to be, and that success in that way is what we should be striving or living for. I grew up with my grandparents and my grandpa was very adamant, "Yes. I support you, we support you in going to school and to college, but you have to remember our way of life and our language, you still have to continue to learn." I remember seeing this poster as a first-year teacher and it said, 'You must read to succeed.' And I just remember feeling like no, that is not true because my parents speak two different languages, my dad comes from the Tewa-speaking tribe of Ohkay Owingeh, formerly known as San Juan Pueblo. They took their name back and that is how they are now known officially. I remember feeling so many times unsuccessful, not good about myself, because Keres or Tewa was not my first language, English was, and I remember being made fun of in my grandpa's village. They would call me "Oh, she's white," or, "She's American because she doesn't speak our language." And then going to Cochiti and the language shift that they had already begun to experience, there was already shame around, if you did know your language, then you were made fun of also. So, I was like the extreme on one side, and then on the other side, and recognising the power of language. So, what Grandma Lily said is that Montessori will help you to assure families that they are going to still get a really good education, a really solid education. We were not worried about English, people are going to learn English no matter what, we were worried about our language surviving. And so, you can get your children to do reading, writing and maths really well, people will feel secure and continue to go back to their own language. And it's not our insecurities around academic success but children who died, people got beaten, they got their mouths washed out with soap. Let's think about my own grandpa who ran away from boarding school three times. These were not places that honoured children, I heard somebody call it a death camp. These were places that were meant to kill our people, starting with the children. What Dr. Suina, one of our elders says is, when the physical wars in the mid-80s stopped, they took that war to our children.

I feel like Montessori helps us to give that sense of security that we can still learn reading, writing and maths in the colonising language of English, but it doesn't have to be at the expense of losing our own.

Charlotte:

That is really well-explained, thank you. The history and the context, as you say, with what happened in the boarding schools was ever-seeking to be an eradication of your language and culture. This is why the program you are doing and many others around the world is so vital, because within a couple of generations, this will be the norm. We would hope that the revitalisation is just a normal part of life, the language immersion programs. And, as you say, with the balance of academics, for those who want the reassurance of academics, but with honouring culture, it is a perfect combination.

4. When was the first time a child taught you something about yourself that you weren't aware of?

Trisha:

I think about all the children that I have had the honour to work with, and I would say probably when I was still at the public school, and had that epiphany that here I was trying to ensure that our daughter spoke Keres as her first language. At Cochiti School, there are non-natives that go there, and then there are also children from the other village that we are from of Kewa Santo Domingo Pueblo. At that time, between 2005 and 2006, there were about three children in my class whose first language was still Keres, and I just remember thinking, "Wow, what a gift that this child is still talking his language. He is smart, and he is working so hard to learn in a second language." He was about six or seven years old, he wasn't asking to teach me or show me anything, but his existence is resistance. I always hear that our existence is resistance. His parents were not framing it like that, but I just think what an amazing job his family had done in ensuring that they continued to talk to him only in Keres. And I just remember feeling that I could not be complicit in the classroom anymore; I didn't believe what I was doing was right anymore, it didn't feel good. And there were a number of these epiphanies, probably starting when I had some of those children whose first language was Keres, but really feeling deeply with my own daughter to make sure she was fluent in our language. Maybe it was cognitive dissonance, like, "Wait, what am I doing? This doesn't make sense. This is not okay." But I think children also show us who we are. Children show us who we are supposed to be if we let them, if we listen, if we observe, as Montessori teaches us to do so well. And who are they? Untouched in so many ways.

If there is a child whose first language is still their Indigenous language, first of all, that is a gift. And second of all, I believe that it is one of the purest forms of who we are as Indigenous people.

The colonising languages, they call them world languages, we need to call them colonising languages because they have devastated the world in so many ways. One of the ways is by not loving, honouring and centring children. In many of our Indigenous cultures, children and survival are at the centre, our languages tell us who we are.

Charlotte:

Language is intrinsically linked to cultural heritage. And, as you say, having the native language as the first language, the mother tongue, and placing that as higher importance than other languages, the importance of that cannot be underestimated. Many people will learn English eventually because that is the dominant language wherever we are in the world for the most part, and I really stress upon parents to speak their mother tongue to their children. Because, as you say, it is tied to their cultural identity and if they are placing English above their own language, then what is that message they are giving to their children?

5. When was the last time a child taught you something about yourself that you weren't aware of?

Trisha:

We have spent the last year learning virtually and were able to keep the KCLC going with both our primary and Elementary classrooms. Our staff has grown from three to sixteen, which is really wonderful. I finally feel like I am at a point where I have a little bit more space to be the teacher that I want to be. Teaching and learning alongside the other co-teacher, Katie Kitchens, the English-speaking guide, and our Keres-speaking Elementary assistant, I am being reminded about why I love to teach and why I do not want to leave the classroom. They remind me why it is so fun and why I enjoy teaching, because you also get to learn beside them.

We did the Pueblo Revolt this year, and they reminded me of how capable, as 11-year-olds, they are learning about our own resistance to the Spaniards and colonisation in 1680, and then connecting that to what is happening now with Black Lives Matter and the racial unrest here in America, and what is happening in Palestine. The connections that they make, they figure out for themselves.

Charlotte:

And that is the gift that we can give the Elementary child because they are in that window of social justice and moral justice. They start to join the dots up and it is so powerful. That is the gift of Montessori, we don't tell them how to think, we give them the keys and they can unlock it.

6. When was the last time a child caught you out of integrity and questioned you on it?

Trisha:

We are a language revitalisation school and it is always a challenge to stay in our language. It is usually me who is reminding the children, "Back to Keres, back to Keres, say what you can in Keres. Oh, I know you know how to say that in Keres." I will be talking in Keres, they will call me by my Keres name, they'll say, "You talked American (meaning English). You are supposed to be talking our language." It does not happen a lot but it does happen. And it's really fun now because they are the ones reminding us and they should be.

7. How did you explain yourself to the children when you were out of integrity?

Trisha:

I want to acknowledge first that our culture and family teaches us to always act with integrity and to be integrated. And what has caused so many people to be disintegrated, and this is not a judgement, is because school separates us into all of these categories, into all of these subjects. I saw somebody make a post asking, how do you use gratitude in your teaching experience? That bothered me, I think that person asked the question with good intent, but it is another reason why we need to support Indigenous languages. Everybody talks about culture. No, it is our language first, and our culture and our worldview, everything is embedded in our languages, and then our languages help us to make the culture stronger.

When we learn, relearn, strengthen and revitalise our culture, it reminds us who we are, how we are supposed to behave, how we are supposed to acknowledge each other and the living world.

I have heard one fellow Cochiti tribal member describe it as our people, our way of life—our language has the highest standards of ethics of how to be a good human being. And again, it is up to us whether we are going to live in those ways, even when it's not convenient for us. One of the things that my grandma really ingrained in us is to be humble, to practice humility. My grandpa insisted that I come home after I went to Stanford University, he said, "Okay, I am so proud of you and I am so honoured and blessed that you are going to graduate, but now it is time to come home." And, so, I just wanted to acknowledge that integrity is always something we are striving for in our everyday lives. When you say out of integrity, we all make mistakes. There is that characteristic of white supremacy culture that is perfectionism. And there are ways in which perfectionism is really unhealthy, it makes people sick because nothing can ever be perfect enough.

I feel like one of the things that probably our ancestors recognised a long time ago is, first of all, nothing is perfect. The only thing that is perfect is Mother Earth, and the land, plants and animals and water. It is humans that are imperfect.

Our elders always say, in our language, that they don't know everything, and that they are open to continuing to learn and to listen, and then integrate it back into our own beliefs and our own values. If it sticks and matches, great. If it doesn't, that's okay. And so, when I make a mistake, I am not afraid to say I have made a mistake, I am not afraid to be corrected. Because if I listen, then it is going to only make me a better human being—children will always make us better teachers, if we choose to listen. Even with my own daughters, the oldest is 17 years old, and the youngest is 14. They remind me when I am not acting in integrity, "Mom, you taught us this but why did you do this?" Or when I recognise that, "You know what girls? This is what I believe, but I see myself doing this, or that, and I want you to understand why." But they are also not afraid to tell me themselves. And as long as we do it respectfully, and we take time to listen, that is how we will continue to grow together. And I feel like our culture, our language, and our elders are really beautiful models of that.

Charlotte:
Firstly, as you said, language is intrinsically linked to culture, we cannot separate the two. We do not want to, and certainly the mother tongue language learning has to be the most important step.

8. What is your favourite Dr. Montessori quote?

Trisha:
My favourite Dr. Montessori quote is: "Of all things, love is the most potent." [1] I have a beautiful picture of our first year of being open at KCLC and it is of my nephew and

another child holding hands on one of our long walks. When I think of that quote, I always think of that really beautiful picture that we captured of them. I am grateful to have come from a family that was so loving, that was able to continue to stay in that space of how we are taught to just love. It is hard to do but I am just grateful for that because it really is true of all things, love is the most potent. And I don't romanticise that because it is too often romanticised and people talk about it, but people don't do it. Because truth is an act of love, justice is an act of love. And how can you do that outside of your family? How can you do that outside of your children? And that is when it matters.

Don't go talking about love, if you cannot do it for other children, if you cannot do it for other people.

9. What is your deepest desire for Montessori for the future?

Trisha:

My deepest desire for Montessori in the future is for Black and Indigenous children, children of colour to have access to it, and in a way that amplifies their own community and their own languages first.

There are so many people that idolise Montessori, hero-worship her and the Montessori approach in a way that is not okay, either - using Montessori education, in service to what the community wants, what we say about Montessori, how we use it in service to our mission of language revitalisation, and not the other way around. Also for Montessori to look at itself, the way in which it is complicit in racism, settler colonialism, and in the oppression of Black, Indigenous children of colour, Asian American Pacific Islanders (AAPI), Mexican Americans, all of the marginalised communities in any settler colonial country, because that has to be reckoned with as well. We have to always remember that we want to use it as service to the community and the children of that community.

Charlotte:

That is really powerful. And in our training, a huge emphasis is placed upon the spiritual preparation of the adult.

10. What do you see is your role in achieving this desire?

Trisha:

I feel like I have been on that journey with helping to co-found KCLC, and I say that I co-founded it because I would not have been able to do it without our Board of

Directors and our tribal council who gave us the blessing to do it. One of the things that our elders tell us is to take time to talk to anybody who comes here to visit and learn from KCLC. We get a lot of visitors, especially from other tribes, not just local, but nationally, and that is why we started our annual symposium. And we also launched the Indigenous Montessori Institute. I really love and appreciate the quote by Dr. Souto Manning, an early childhood Professor out of Columbia Teachers College, who talks about the ways in which teacher training programs are deeply implicated in the perpetuation of white supremacy culture. In order to fundamentally transform what teachers are doing and what education is doing, we have to transform teacher training. And so, for us at KCLC, we already knew that we needed our teachers to be trained in language immersion techniques, dual language education, and of course, Montessori. We couldn't just send them to The University of New Mexico (UNM) or the Community College in New Mexico (CNM) or Santa Fe Community College, because then we would have to deprogram them. We recognised that we have to create this teacher training centre ourselves, so it is a shared work at KCLC, with our Directors, our administrators, our elders, all of our staff and our families. I feel like we are doing our part.

Charlotte:

If we are going to change the way that children's futures are shaped, we have to start with the way that teachers are trained. It makes perfect sense, we cannot put teachers into a colonised system and expect them to be able to then celebrate Indigenous culture. The Indigenous Montessori Institute is a powerful vehicle for change.

Trisha:

We are a not-for-profit and have been from the beginning because we did not want to accept funding from the state or federal government that would tie us to testing in English, which competes with our mission. Donations help to keep us open and help keep us afloat. We always appreciate any support that we receive, even if it's prayers, even if it's amplification, making space for us, just as you have Charlotte. Thank you for not being complicit and for making sure that you had an Indigenous person from the settler colonial United States. Thank you for supporting our children.

Charlotte:

Thank you so much. It has really been a great pleasure to learn from you and from all the wisdom you bring.

Lifting Hearts off the Ground

Declaring Indigenous Rights in Poetry
LYLA JUNE JOHNSTON AND JOY DE VITO [2]

On any given day you can
find Trisha Moquino working
in the classroom, cultivating
little seeds with bright brown eyes,
smiles so wide, open minds, open hands.
They speak their dreams to the daylight
in the Keres language.

She is nourishing their minds,
their bodies, their speech.
Linguistic diversity in the age of extinction.
Like the cottonwood trees,
like the rare desert rivers, prayer births
the sustainability of genes and languages.

Those who seek conquest
have their backs turned to her.
They are lost in business,
busy-ness, busy building
a cemetery for the unborn.
When will they stop
and help her plant the seeds?
When will they see it is time to nourish
what their grandparents worked so hard
to destroy? Even dead soil can be
revived when we work together.

A peek into the world of Trisha

Images: From top, left to right
(1) Montessori for Social Justice 2018 **(2)** Painting by Trish's elder daughter **(3)** Language lesson with Percy. **(4)** Trisha in class 2012 **(5)** Figurine made by Trisha's great Aunt from Cochiti Pueblo **(6)** Kawaika B-Day Circle 2014 **(7)** Necklace made by Trisha's Grandpa

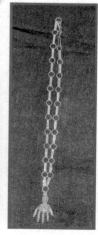

Reflective practice

1. Journal

"Children show us who we are supposed to be if we let them, if we listen, if we observe, as Montessori teaches us to do so well. And who are they? Untouched in so many ways. If there is a child whose first language is still their Indigenous language, first of all, that is a gift. And second of all, I believe that it is one of the purest forms of who we are as Indigenous people." **Trisha Moquino (2021)**

Trisha spoke extensively and passionately about her mission to revitalise and prioritise the languages of Indigenous communities. She works tirelessly to prioritise Indigenous languages above colonising settler languages that have been forced on to Indigenous communities throughout history. With this in mind, your journal prompts are:

- Consider what language you use in everyday life to communicate with your family, your child, your friends, and to the wider public. Do you speak in your mother tongue? Is the language you speak the dominant language of where you reside? If not, do you speak the local language?
- How does language enrich your culture? If your language was taken from you, how would this impact on your culture, and how you interact and connect with your community?
- Now consider how this loss of language and culture could impact your child. How would you show them your values and beliefs without the language that they are embedded in?

2. Embodiment

"I want to acknowledge first that our culture and family teaches us to always act with integrity and to be integrated... I have heard one fellow Cochiti tribal member describe it as our people, our way of life, our language has the highest standards of ethics, of how to be a good human being. And again, it is up to us whether we are going to live in those ways, even when it's not convenient for us." **Trisha Moquino (2021)**

Trisha speaks of the highest standards of integrity that are the core of her people and their values.

With this in mind, for your embodiment practice reflect upon the following:

- What are the standards of integrity in your culture, religion or community that you practise and role model to your children? What do these standards of integrity feel like to you?
- How does it feel in your body when you are acting in integrity? Where is this sensation located?
- How does it feel in your body when you are acting out of integrity? Where is this sensation located?

3. Creativity

"For me, any light bulb moment has always, first and foremost, been in the way that the philosophy aligns with our philosophy of children. Because the way that has been imposed on our people, as Indigenous peoples, and there are over 572 tribes that are still in existence today, has always been to centre English, and has tried, as General Pratt, the founder of the military boarding schools said, "Kill the Indian, save the man."
'With Montessori, I saw an opportunity for us to support our language and culture. Also, the way in which she recognises the spirit of the child and does not try to separate that."
Trisha Moquino (2021)

Indigenous communities all over the world have been fighting against erasure from colonisers for centuries. I invite you to consider how the eradication of their languages and land continues today and how you can respectfully honour these communities through self-reflection, learning and taking action.

You may wish to consider, as a starting point, whether the land you currently live on is colonised land? If so, who does this land originally belong to? If it is Indigenous land, is there a Land Acknowledgment which recognises this? (As a first step to acknowledging Native land, there is a useful resource at https://native-land.ca/)

- How does your research about the people of this land enrich your knowledge about their culture, language, traditions, music, dance and art?
- What can you do with your child to honour the first people of the land on which you now reside?

Share your thoughts... Email me sayhello@enrichingenvironments.com. Join me on Instagram & Facebook , follow me, tag my profile @enrichingenvironments and use the hashtag #montessorimission

CHAPTER 5

Barbara Isaacs

As a Montessori Granny, President of Montessori Europe and Co-Founder of Montessori Musings, Barbara Isaacs is encouraging current and new generations of parents and Educators in searching for the essence of childhood. Through her work, Barbara nurtures the joy of play and learning, trust and respect for all children and communities, with love and care for the riches of our beautiful planet.

A passionate, dignified and unifying voice for an inclusive and diverse Montessori practice, Barbara Isaacs has spent more than three decades working with Montessori students and the Montessori academic faculty at St. Nicholas, London Montessori Centre, and Montessori Centre International (MCI). She has had the privilege of running a nursery school, training Montessori teachers and leading a team of knowledgeable and dedicated Montessori colleagues in developing new courses. She has published a magazine, written articles and a couple of books, has organised conferences, and represented Montessori at government and international level. Her two children, and more recently her two granddaughters, have also benefited from what she has gained from all of these professional and personal experiences. Together with a friend, Barbara publishes the Montessori Granny blog and contributes to My Montessori Life podcasts.

I met Barbara whilst studying for my 3-6 diploma at MCI in London, 2011. My lecture room was next to Barbara's office and I soon realised that if I got in early, I would be able to sneak in 10 magical minutes with her to talk about Montessori while she sipped her cup of tea. Those chats were a great inspiration to me and the catalyst to me teaching in Cape Town. I am so grateful for the inspiration, guidance and encouragement Barbara has offered and continues to offer me for over a decade.

The Montessori Mission, by Charlotte Awdry

We begin the 10 Questions...

1. What does Montessori mean to you?

Barbara:

Without any doubt, it means the connection with the child. The thing that attracted me to Montessori in the first place was her huge reverence for the potential of the child, and the fact that she invites us to trust and respect children. This still remains the motivator for the work that I do,

I believe that if we can change the life of one child, and that child feels more respected and revered by the community around them, then we have made a difference.

Recently, we have come to revisit her social impact writing and talk about the importance of interdependence and solidarity, and the role education plays in changing the world. But we need to start with the very young child at the very beginning, in the first six years of life. This is the age group that I have really loved working with, and I still continue to enjoy observing and learning through my granddaughters.

2. What was your first light bulb moment on your Montessori path?

Barbara:

Initially, when I first trained, I was so inspired by the prepared environment, by the amazing materials that she thought so deeply about, and played such an important role in the child's development. I just loved the idea of learning a little bit more about the cultural area of the classroom. When I trained this was quite neglected and we often just referred to the globes and to the Sensorial experiences of this area of learning. But in the last 35 years this area of the Montessori environment has developed greatly, and it has given us an opportunity to really look beyond the materials. It has given us an opportunity to look at the essence of Montessori, the concept of global citizenship, and the very strong connections with nature and with the rest of the world. As I progressed in my Montessori training, I became more strongly connected with the cultural materials and the potential they give us to share the world with young children. It is very important for me to make young children feel that they are part of the earth and part of the universe.

When I set up a nursery there were a couple of moments which really showed me that I needed to see the children in a different way. On one occasion, I was showing a mother around whilst her two-year-old son was exploring the environment. It was his first visit to the Montessori learning environment, and in those days we kept the four-cylinder blocks organised in a square, on a mat on the floor. He sat by the cylinders, took them all out and put them all back. This taught me that we need to watch the child and how they engage with the materials before we begin to do presentations. For this child, it would have been totally pointless to say, "I've got something exciting to show you," and bring one cylinder block. He had already tackled all four, and was able to sort them out in the right holes, showing that one-to-one correspondence in the cylinders. So, that was the first step when I began to think about the materials in a different way, the need to really see what the child can do first with the material before presenting my version of how to use them.

The second moment was when I was studying for my Master's. I was exploring the ideas of extensions of the Sensorial material, and the relationship between work and play in Montessori settings. We had one girl in the nursery who really loved the pink tower. I was filming her and she was doing it so perfectly, and at the end, I said to her, "What else would you like to do with the pink tower?" She looked at me as if to say, "What else should I do? I have done what you showed me." In the Sensorial materials or the Practical Life activities, the child will probably work out how it works, or they may show you a new way, which you have never seen. For me, the light bulb moments were that we must continue to learn from children in the same way as Montessori learned from children when she first set up her nursery.

It made me think about the nature of the Montessori teacher training, and why we train in that way. Why is there so much emphasis on the use of the materials? I have witnessed this very rigid approach to the sequence of the materials and to the volume in the planned activities that teachers have for children. Teachers expect that the children will do what they want them to do.

Montessori talks about the fact that you will not always get it right, that you will not always match the children's needs and need for spontaneous engagement to what you think they may be ready for. And what you think they may be ready for is very different to the way we have been taught the sequence of the Montessori materials and how we organise the environment. The child must be free to show us their need, to show us their interest by the way they approach the shelves and what they take off the shelves.

My granddaughter really loved building towers and knocking them down for many months. But whenever I offered her a Montessori piece of material she would absolutely refuse. And that has been a real lesson to me as a Montessorian—the need to stand back and see what the child is telling us in their actions. And to be humble

The Montessori Mission, by Charlotte Awdry

enough to accept the child's mode of learning, because they need to feel that their ideas are valued, which to me is this idea of respect.

Children need to feel settled and have a sense of belonging if they are ready to benefit from a Montessori environment or any environment where they encounter other adults.

3. In what ways does Montessori enrich the work that you do?

Barbara:

It enriches me every single day when I think of the understanding I have gained of children through my study, continued learning and having dialogue with students, colleagues and friends over the years. It always reminds me of this reverence for the child. I am so fortunate to be able to contribute in very small ways to the lives of children today, and particularly to continue to learn about children through my two granddaughters, which is a huge gift. I don't always give it the Montessori label but her words are in my heart.

I have been so encouraged to spend time reading Montessori Speaks to Parents (2017), which is a booklet that came out recently, and it is incredibly accessible to parents. It says everything about our relationship with the child that I really believe and endorse. I would like every parent to read it, so that they can get a glimpse or more of an understanding of who their child is and to accept their child for who they are. It is very difficult for us, as parents and grandparents, not to try to mould the child just a tiny bit, according to what is important to us. But I try to remember every single day that I am with my grandchildren, to be there with them and for them, to feel the day with them and be in the moment. Being a grandparent really gives you that opportunity to be in the moment.

And I think that if we can help children to articulate their feelings and accept all of their emotions, not just the moments of joy and happiness, but also understand that they need to have an opportunity to let out their frustrations, anger, jealousy and disappointment, that all of these feelings are part of childhood. If we are there with them for those moments, it is more likely that they will come to understand their own emotions and will be able to speak about them. In Philippa Perry's book 'The Book You Wish Your Parents Had Read (and Your Children Will Be Glad That You Did)' (2020), she she speaks of how she worked hard to help their daughter to articulate all of her feelings, particularly the feelings of anger and frustration. This made it possible for her mother to say during those difficult moments, "Yes, I can see that this is very annoying, let's talk about it." When the child loses control because they cannot articulate how they feel, and the parent then tries to fix it, this often makes the child even more angry and frustrated.

Charlotte:

Or the child has a tantrum, and then the adult has their own tantrum.

Barbara:

And it's not helpful to the child if you have a tantrum, because then they do not feel contained. They do not feel that there is somebody there who is helping them to manage their emotions.

Charlotte:

They do not get any emotional safety from that and they need lots and lots of emotional safety so they can, as you said, release and feel safe. And then they can start to unpick it over time and start to predict when things are going a bit wobbly for themselves, but it is a long process.

Barbara:

Also, as a parent, you cannot get it 100% right, there will be moments when you lose it too. What is important is for the parent or adult to then go back and say, "I'm really sorry, I didn't manage that well, I was not really helpful."

Charlotte:

I think the humility in being able to apologise to our child and admit when we were not able to be the best version of ourselves is really powerful. To understand that we are immensely complex as humans, and when we do make a mistake to be able to hold our hands up. That is such powerful role modelling for our children to know that we are not expecting them to get it right the whole time because we are owning that we do not get it right. That feels like a big generational leap.

Barbara:

It is a big leap, but it also helps to alleviate the adult guilt, because when you lose it as an adult, you feel incredibly guilty for your lack of competence. And being able to say, "I'm really sorry, I have not managed that well," in a way eases the situation for you as an adult too.

4. When was the first time a child taught you something about yourself that you weren't aware of?

Barbara:

It happened when our daughter was about four and her brother was coming up to two. I was finding parenting really tricky and went to parenting classes where I came to understand lots of things from my own childhood. In particular a game I used to play with my brother after our father died suddenly in hospital. In the game I was the parent and my brother was an ill child who went to hospital but would always recover. It was a perpetual game that we played for many years, and of course, 60 years ago people did not quite understand the repercussions of the game and there was very little support for bereavement.

But as a result of those childhood experiences, I have always felt that I needed to fix everything for my daughter, that I needed to make her life easier so that she would not struggle. What I learned in those parenting classes was that not everything is of my making, that I need her to be herself.

Even though Montessori talks about the fact that we need to accept each child for who they are, and we need to respect them, it is much more challenging when you are a parent and feel deeply emotionally connected with your child, you really do want their life to be better than yours. And that is a real challenge of parenting!

But learning that I cannot fix everything was very, very important for me, and I would not have learned it if it wasn't for the challenges that parenting two children presented me with.

5. When was the last time a child taught you something about yourself that you weren't aware of?

Barbara:

It was my older granddaughter. I went to visit a Nido in London and there was this wonderful activity where children could put toothpicks through a little hole, and I saw this one-year-old doing it so beautifully, I was so impressed. So, I quickly prepared this for my new granddaughter, and put it on the table thinking that she would be so curious. She took one look at it, as if to say: "What are you thinking about?" She was totally not interested and has continued to refuse Montessori activities.

It is so easy to slip into the teacher role. We had some silicone cupcake cases in different colours, and she was playing with them. I said, "Shall we sort them out by colour?" And I started doing it and she very quickly muddled them up and said, "Actually, this is the field for my cow, she can eat all this wonderful grass and all the flowers," and then she brought this stuffed cow and put it next to the cupcake cases! I am really being taught by my grandchildren to rethink my role as an Educator and I am continuously challenged in the value of the Montessori materials. The thing that really first attracted me to Montessori and what I so loved in the beginning, are that these are tools for learning which I still value hugely. But I question if they still mean as much to the children of today, as they did in her day. I think as Montessorians, we really need to question the activities that we put out for children on the shelves and what they give to them.

We need to think about the fact that if we continue to perpetuate this authentic Montessori environment, which is not touched by the culture or background of the children with whom we are working, then that in itself becomes a tool for perpetuating this white colonial influence.

In training, we should be able to help our students understand the principles behind the materials, so that they have the capacity to recreate similar activities, even when working with communities. For example, in refugee camps or in communities where there is no access to these resources. If we really want Montessori to become the tool for learning for children around the world, we need to grapple with those issues.

Charlotte:
It has to be accessible in a different way, culturally, racially, and economically accessible. Not to just ship them in or have them donated from another school.

Barbara:
The worst thing for me is when a school takes the things they do not wish to use anymore but are still usable, and gives them as a gesture of great generosity to children who have nothing. I think those children deserve the most pristine materials we can offer them because they have nothing, and it enables us to show our respect for them.

Charlotte:
And whatever we offer, it has to be culturally relevant. It can't be, as you say, the white colonial model, because we are just perpetuating elitism if we do that.

Barbara:
It is also in the way we share the preparation of the environment and how we train our teachers; it is a much bigger issue. We need teachers who thoroughly understand the materials, embrace the philosophy and continue to be sensitive to the culture.

Charlotte:
In that great film, Inside Montessori (Quiet Island Films, 2019) the Principal of one of the schools says children need a mirror and a window, people who look like them, and

then a window out to the world. And that just still sticks with me so deeply, it is so important.

Barbara:

When I was reflecting on the new regulation for earliest education in the UK, I went back to the analogy of mirrors and windows. We have to offer the mirror for the child to see themselves in their community, in our environment, but also open the doors to the world.

> **To be the sliding door between the window and the mirror is such a privilege, we are really enabling children to see themselves and the rest of the world. For me, that still remains at the heart of Montessori.**

I still see that as the roots of global citizenship, I see that as the value of the whole philosophy and the idea of cosmic education.

6. When was the last time a child caught you out of integrity and questioned you on it?

Barbara:

I don't know if it caught me out of integrity, but when my four-year-old granddaughter asked the question, "When there were no humans, how could the babies grow inside mommy's tummy?" I was unprepared and unable to answer it to my own satisfaction. It is such a demonstration of the young child's capacity for deep thinking and to ask really big questions that we often shy away from. I thought that she was ready for the story of life and I would try to explain it to her but, of course when I tried to return to the question two days later with her, it was no longer of interest. And this is why it is so very important that the adult agenda never overrides the child's question, because if you lose that moment, you may never come back to it because whilst it lingers with you as an adult, the child moves on.

7. How did you explain yourself when you were out of integrity?

Barbara:

I said, "We are just creatures in the animal kingdom, like all other creatures, and there were other creatures before us." That was my idea to prepare her for the story of life. I was ready to go into the history of the prehistoric timeline, or the first story of the Earth. It's still there in the back of my mind, I dug out the book, and now I'm prepared. If the question comes again, I can say, "I can show you, shall we look at this together?" And we will see what comes.

Charlotte:

I like your answer, "There were other creatures here before us." That was all she needed to know at that moment.

Barbara:

I think that in all of those answers, you need to be authentic. You need to say the things that you really believe in because they very quickly suss out when you are being disingenuous, they know when you are just kidding them.

I must share this little anecdote from my life. So, the approach that we have always had with our children is if the children asked something and we didn't quite know, we would say, "Well, let's find out." So, my daughter came from school at the age of eight and said, "Now I know all about sexual intercourse." I said, "That's very interesting. How did you come upon this?" And she said, "Well, somebody mentioned it in class and I didn't know what it was. I went into the library and I looked it up in the dictionary." For me, that was absolutely empowering, giving the autonomy to the child, giving access to knowledge. She knew how to use the tools that we had given her a long time ago, I shouldn't have been surprised.

Charlotte:

She didn't know the answer so she went and found out for herself.

Barbara:

She knew what to do and went to the best source at that moment in time, because it satisfied her curiosity, and she was comfortable because she then came home and shared it.

8. What is your favourite Dr. Montessori quote?

Barbara:

At this moment it is the quote from Montessori Speaks to Parents: "The greatest help you can give them (children) is to stand by and see that they are free to develop in their own way." [1] This resonates with me and embodies the biggest challenge for parents and Educators – to let the child be free to develop in their own way – to be themselves. In the same book Montessori talks about the child keeping secrets, the idea that the secret of childhood lies within the child and we, as adults, can only guess. Hopefully the more we know, the better the guess will be, but how the child thinks and how they absorb information really remains a secret.

The Montessori Mission, by Charlotte Awdry

We need to be very diligent observers through observing their responses and body language, so we are able to accept them for who they really are.

My quest in life is to continue to learn about children, to accept that each child is different and therefore what I have learned from one child may change for the next one, but not always. It reminds us of the need for humility, patience, and to accept the child for who they are, which is probably the biggest challenge for us as adults.

9. What is your deepest desire for Montessori in the future?

Barbara:

I would like the Montessori community to free themselves of the need to review the materials and to instead go back to Dr. Montessori's writing to continue to reflect on what she says. Because when I read Montessori texts 35 years ago as a student, I had a very, very different understanding. We interpret the reading in the context of our own experience, and therefore returning to the text and grappling with it at the point where we are at the moment is really important. And I don't mean just reading the text, because of course we are always inspired. But sometimes we are also challenged because of the use of language and because some of the ideas that she shares with us have now been explored in developmental psychology and in other areas. So, we need to combine the two together to see how they work in real life. As a community, if we want to demonstrate that Montessori pedagogy has value in the 21st century, it will not be through the materials, it will be through helping people to understand the spirit of the child and really see the child as a potential agent of social change.

Charlotte:

What is really amazing when talking to Montessorians from around the world, in different situations and different communities, is how everyone comes back to the importance of the spirit of the child, not the materials or even the environment, it is the spirit of the child. I think that is really powerful because it shows that we are all on the same page.

10. What do you see is your role in achieving this desire?

Barbara:

I feel very fortunate because even though I have retired, an opportunity has presented itself for me to be able to collaborate, connect and engage with other Montessorians through Zoom. I think it's amazing that technology has given us this opportunity. I will always be a teacher. I pretended to be a teacher when I was six years old in my role play and I am still a teacher even though it came as a second profession to me. Being a teacher means that you continue to learn, and so I need to continue to learn about myself, I need to continue to learn about other people. I think that all of the different voices that we have heard from the Montessori community during the recent years, which were suddenly made available to us because of technology, has encouraged us to continue to discuss, explore and participate in a dialogue about what Montessori means.

I would like people to engage more with the heart of play, and what play means to children, in a much more positive way than is sometimes seen in Montessori circles. I think that sometimes we focus too much on work and forget that the child's play is their work, and that it is through play that we really see the soul of the child.

I have not been able to see the soul of the child through building the pink tower! But I have been able to see the child in a different way, by observing their play, which is often much more enriching and tells me so much more about the child's culture and how they relate to others.

For me, preschool education is about learning to be a social being and therefore we need to give the child opportunities to develop their whole self through play. What holds us back is our connection with the materials when, in fact, Montessori never wrote a manual on how to use the materials. She said, "You present it to the child and then you let the child use the materials." That has become the biggest challenge of the Montessori community today, we expect them to use the materials in the way we have presented them, and this is why I think we need to move away from presenting the materials first. We need to start by looking at what the child can do with the materials and then use what we have learned from that to either present it in a formal way, or offer other things which would extend that capacity to learn.

Play gives the children full control of the scenario. Whereas being in a classroom, no matter how nurturing it is for the child, they are, to some extent, working to other people's expectations. And children want to be liked by their teachers, so they will do things for their teachers much more than they will ever do for you as a parent. But because they have contained who they really are in order to present themselves to the other adult in a positive light, when they come home, they need to let it out.

Charlotte:
Harry does it every single day. In the classroom I hear from his Guide that he is the model of Practical Life, he cleans up after everyone else, puts everything back where it belongs on the shelf. But when he comes home, he needs to be a real four-year-old and let it all out.

Barbara:

I witnessed with my own children how important the nursery years in the Montessori environment and the Montessori principles are. When they went to Elementary school, I became concerned about the influence of other children and the lack of challenge in the mainstream educational system.

However, when they came to Secondary school, I suddenly saw that all of the values, the things that we had planted as part and parcel of being a family, which they had internalised, became their own. I began to see them unfolding into really caring and considerate human beings.

The biggest gift in my life was to learn about Montessori before my children were born, so I could give them this beginning. It wasn't perfect, and I am sure that if you spoke to them, they would all have their own interpretation of it. But it has helped them to become who they are today and they are very decent human beings. I really value that because, as parents, that is the only gift we can give to our children.

Images: (left) *Our children – Adelle and Danny who have benefited from my Montessori training and, to this day I feel they are the biggest gift life has bestowed on me.* **(Right)** *Children from Seedlings Montessori Nursery, Oxfordshire, set up by myself and a friend in 1991. A dream come true enabling me to nurture 'global citizenship' through projects such as the dressing up suitcase which served as a folding activity to inspire "travel and experiences" beyond the very homogeneous market town community*

On Children

KHALIL GIBRAN[2]

And a woman who held a babe against her bosom said,
Speak to us of Children.

And he said:
Your children are not your children.
They are the sons and daughters of Life's longing for itself.
They come through you but not from you,
And though they are with you yet they belong not to you.

You may give them your love but not your thoughts,
For they have their own thoughts.
You may house their bodies but not their souls,
For their souls dwell in the house of tomorrow,
which you cannot visit, not even in your dreams.

You may strive to be like them, but seek not to make them like you.
For life goes not backward nor tarries with yesterday.
You are the bows from which your children as living arrows are sent forth.
The archer sees the mark upon the path of the infinite, and He bends you
with His might that His arrows may go swift and far.

Let your bending in the archer's hand be for gladness;
For even as He loves the arrow that flies,
so He loves also the bow that is stable.

Barbara: I chose this passage from Kahlil Gibran's Prophet which embodies
the biggest challenge for parents and Educators – to let the child be free to
develop in their own way – to be themselves.

A peek into the world of Barbara

Images: From top, left to right

(1) Artwork by Czech artist friend, celebrating the Velvet revolution, ending a communist regime in the Czech republic that changed lives for the country and my family. **(2)** Graduation of Syrian refugees in Lebanon. **(3)** Tanya – her family gave me a home when I first came to England. Tanya and her dad inspired me to consider retraining to be a Montessori teacher at the age of 33. **(4)** Celebrating Montessori training with Tibetan refugee women at Norbulinka Creche, Dharamsala, India. The most humbling experience of my teaching career. **(5)** Celebrating the end of a St. Nicholas workshop – the first one I helped to deliver to Montessori distance learning students, from whom I learned so much in the early days of my teaching career.

Reflective practice

1. Journal

"To be the sliding door between the window and the mirror is such a privilege, we are really enabling children to see themselves and the rest of the world. For me, that still remains at the heart of Montessori. I still see that as the roots of global citizenship, I see that as the value of the whole philosophy and the idea of cosmic education."
Barbara Isaacs (2021)

For Barbara, global citizenship is the essence of Montessori and she encourages us to look beyond the materials in order to share the world with our child, for them to explore their connection with others and the natural world, and feel a strong sense of belonging wherever they are. With this in mind, journal upon the following questions:

- What does it mean to you to be a global citizen?
- How are you raising your children to be global citizens?

2. Embodiment

"(We have) an opportunity to look at the essence of Montessori, the concept of global citizenship and the very strong connections with nature and with the rest of the world. As I progressed in my Montessori training, I became more strongly connected with the cultural materials and the potential they give us to share the world with young children. It is very important for me to make young children feel that they are part of the earth and part of the universe." **Barbara Isaacs (2021)**

How would it feel within you to expand into this vision of us all being interconnected as global citizens? When we remove the political borders imposed by governments, we are all one people, inextricably linked on this beautiful planet we call home. I invite you to close your eyes and ground your feet into the earth. Take this moment to think about what it means to be a global citizen and notice how this FEELS within your body.

Allow yourself to feel this deep connection to others as the sensations travel up your body. This connection could present itself to you as light, energy, billions of tiny strands or through the power of God, whichever way it comes to you, feel this deep affinity to others.

It might also feel good to move your body, to dance, sway or flow. Consider how this movement expands your feeling of interconnectedness, making it a whole body experience.

Can you now radiate this feeling of interconnectedness out of your body, and extend it to friends, family, to people in a country you have never visited, someone whose life is very different from your own. Feel your connection to these strangers, to people all around the world.

The next step is to explore this feeling of interconnectedness with your child, creating a shared experience with them of what it feels like to be a global citizen. This could be through creating a mind map of all of the people and places that we are connected with.

3. Creativity

"The child's play is their work and that it is through play that we really see the soul of the child. I have been able to see the child in a different way, by observing their play, which tells me so much about the child's culture and how they relate to others."
Barbara Isaacs (2021)

In Barbara's hopes for the future she spoke of parents and educators understanding the importance of play, and how through play we see the soul of the child. I invite you to welcome this notion of play into your daily life as an adult. Playing just for the sake of playing, creating for the purpose of creating in the way that a young child does, with no agenda or end goal.

What does this look like for you? How would you like to play? How would you like to create? Think about your own experiences in nature and how nature can be an inspiration for play. How do you and your child connect with nature and creativity? This could be lying on the beach, looking up at the clouds, or sitting on the grass watching the sun rise, familiarising yourself with the plants, flowers and wildlife in your local area, exploring parks and public spaces around you to find out what is unique about them. What ideas of play do these experiences in nature invoke in you?

Share your thoughts... Email me sayhello@enrichingenvironments.com. Join me on Instagram & Facebook , follow me, tag my profile @enrichingenvironments and use the hashtag #montessorimission

CHAPTER 6

Aziza Osman

Of Syrian heritage, raised in the Netherlands, now living in Dubai, Aziza is the Founder of Montiplay, a company that provides parents access to the unique and powerful learning method of Montessori at home by delivering the tools and guidance they need at every developmental stage.

Aziza is a human development professional with 10 years of experience in designing education access solutions using technology, and has a Masters in Public Administration specialising in early childhood education policy and migration. This experience and desire to improve the lives of children led her to found Montiplay, whose mission is to provide access to education for every child, especially those less fortunate and in marginalised communities. They aim to help provide refugee children with a safe and stable learning environment amidst the chaos, and each purchase from Montiplay helps provide for a child less fortunate.

Aziza and I first met in February 2020 here in Dubai and we have since become firm friends. Aziza can really be credited with creating this beautiful, nurturing Montessori community of like-minded Educators and parents here in the Middle East, which did not exist when I first came to Dubai seven years ago. It is so wonderful to have a champion for Montessori in the Arab world; she is really bringing Montessori to the forefront of conversations here and bringing the joy of Montessori into people's homes.

We begin the 10 Questions...

1. What does Montessori mean to you?

Aziza:

For me, Montessori is relearning everything in life but correctly and more clearly this time. It is the manual to building, creating and maintaining relationships, to communicate our emotions proactively. It is the manual to taking care of ourselves, physically, mentally and emotionally, taking care of others and taking care of our environment. Ultimately, Montessori to me means leading a balanced life with purposefulness, to be confident, to become a prepared adult that is able to then raise, enable and empower a smaller human being. This not only applies to the soft skills but also to the academic parts, it's relearning how we learn language, mathematics, science, and being confident that this methodology is science-backed and is time-tested.

Charlotte:

Montessori speaks so much about the spiritual preparation of the adult. As we travel on the Montessori path, the parenting path, it becomes more apparent that our spiritual preparation is really what matters because we can be anywhere in the world and be a Montessorian and practice peace education at its core.

Aziza:

It makes so much sense to apply the Montessori principles to ourselves before we attempt to apply Montessori to our children. It really is a personal journey for the adult before it is something that can be applied as a parent.

2. What was your first light bulb moment on your Montessori journey?

Aziza:

I have two. The first was when my daughter was four months old and had started becoming more aware. Seeing her awake for more hours of the day, I started researching what I could do to effectively and supportively acknowledge her development. When I started reading the books, my first light bulb moment was that I could have started Montessori from conception or birth. I had my own prejudices and preconceptions that Montessori was for preschool children, three years onwards. I had missed out! That was my first light bulb moment, that you could actually start practising Montessori at conception, or when the child is older, or even as an adult who wants to become prepared. Montessori can be applied at any point in time. My second light bulb moment was reading all about Montessori. I realised that it all comes down to putting ourselves in the place of the child, putting ourselves in their shoes, looking at the world around us from their perspective.

3. What ways does Montessori enrich the work that you do?

Aziza:

Montessori provided me with the confidence that I noticed was lacking in myself and moms around me, which is the confidence that we are doing the right thing and we are doing right by our children.

With Montessori I believe that I have gained confidence in the way that I parent, it has given me the self-love that I needed to go on the parenting journey. Following a lifestyle that is science-backed, time-tested, that has endured and survived and proven itself over and over again, really has given me the confidence that I needed in my work and in my life.

Charlotte:

The key is giving parents permission to trust their inner wisdom because we have all the answers we need inside ourselves. Our work is to say to parents, "You can trust yourself, your instincts are there, block out the noise from the outside world. You know this because you observe your child, you spend hours with them." That is what I love about Dr. Montessori's work; she reassures us that anyone can do this, just observe your child, look at your child. All of us have this knowledge and it's just our work to find the right key for the lock for parents.

4. When was the first time a child taught you something about yourself that you weren't aware of?

Aziza:

I was able to realise this because of Montessori and through self-reflecting. When Layla started forming words, I wanted to enrich her language and practice with her as much as possible. Our language of communication at home was Arabic, but I was switching to English when outside of our home. The first time I observed this about myself, I tried to evaluate why this was the case. Why do I attempt to speak a language in front of others and try to perfect the accent? To show that I am equal or on par with the outside world? To not feel like a second-class citizen, the way I did growing up as a child in Europe, when I felt embarrassed speaking Arabic or maintaining our culture? Switching languages with Layla was one of my first moments of realisation that I should be speaking only one with her to ensure that it develops quickly.

The Montessori Mission, by Charlotte Awdry

This moment of realisation really made me reflect on the adult that I want to be around my child, and the confidence I need to have in myself, so that she is able to have that confidence as a child and as she grows into an adult.

Montessori is very capable of making us realise that the shortcomings we have today are because of certain events in our childhood. And then how we can grow or heal our inner child, so that we don't project these shortcomings or these feelings of insecurity onto our children. I think of my lack of confidence as a shortcoming or wound on an ongoing journey. I still haven't healed the wound, it is an ongoing process.

Charlotte:

Thank you for sharing so vulnerably about that. It is something that resonates with every Arab family I work with, trying to place English higher on the scale than the richness of your culture, language and heritage.

5. When was the last time a child taught you something about yourself that you weren't aware of?

Aziza:

I recently enrolled for an AMI certification and the prerequisite was many hours of classroom observation. Sitting in a Montessori environment and observing children, I realised that we all come with a lot of prejudices, judgments and some preconceptions that we form one way or another. As adults, we all carry prejudices, whether they come from our families or our upbringing, or the stories we are told as children about others. Our role as prepared adults is to be able to rid ourselves of these prejudices, of these judgments, and to be able to practice observing as objectively as possible. The practice of objectivity and observing with an open mind and an open heart.

6. When was the last time a child called you out on integrity and questioned you on it?

Aziza:

We are a work in progress. I know that we should never be dishonest with our children, and of course, honesty is one of the core principles and values that we try to add to harness hope in our children. However, when we want to leave the house, I open the door and I say, "Layla, the door is gonna close if you don't come, if we don't get out in time." I'm not leaving without her and she knows that and calls me out on it. The look in her eyes makes me realise that it is not working, it is like rewards and punishments and many other things that just do not work, it is not effective. And so, I just take a deep breath, get down to her level and say, "We really need to leave home right now and put on our shoes, so that we can go to school and meet our friends and continue our day." She listens to me and knows that I am not going anywhere without her.

The way that she looks at me makes me realise how ineffective these conditional statements are, and that we need to practice being in control of these moments. This is one of the biggest struggles for me in becoming a prepared adult, to practice being fully honest with my child in these moments.

What is the better approach, so that my child won't look at me in such a way and call me out on my dishonesty in this situation? The trigger brings back the old methods. It is a work in progress on our Montessori journey to realise these triggers and not go back to old methods of parenting, but switch to more conscious parenting methods of honesty and transparency with our children at all times.

Charlotte:
Thank you for answering so honestly. It is not possible for all of us to respond from the best version of ourselves every single time. When we are looking at the conscious parenting method, or the Montessori parenting method, the number one thing is our connection. What can we do to elicit cooperation through connection? We can achieve this but with great big lorry loads of self-compassion, because we are not going to get it right every time.

8. What is your favourite Dr. Montessori quote?

Aziza:
The latest one is "From the depth of his nature, the child repeatedly pardons the adult and strives to flourish despite the latter's repressions" [1].

This quote is powerful in so many ways because it is a relief, it takes a lot of weight off of me as a parent. But it is also heartbreaking that these little humans struggle to really make it on their own when we do not provide them with the right support. You can only imagine if we did not hold them back what they would be able to accomplish. So, with all that we do, with all of these ineffective methods that we use on them, with all the repression, the child will flourish regardless. As Dr. Maria Montessori puts it, they reincarnate themselves. They will flourish, they will reveal themselves and unfold to be the person that they are meant to be. I would love to write this quote down and have it hung somewhere, to have a constant reminder that I should not be the person that is holding her back in any way. I should be the support, like the scaffolding in a building.

The Montessori Mission, by Charlotte Awdry

So, I try as much as possible to be that source of support for her and not be the person that is holding her back.

9. What is your deepest desire for Montessori in the future?

Aziza:

My deepest desire is that Montessori becomes the norm in every household, in every family, in every country, in every nation around the world. It is my mission for it to become accessible and be the lifestyle that we all follow. But, most importantly, that the principles and values in Montessori become a norm, especially when it comes to peace education, when it comes to letting go of our prejudices and our preconceptions of others.

For us to be a stronger global community, we need to embody these values and principles in our lives.

I do believe that we can make that wish come true and realise that goal today with more people around the world, like yourself and the many Montessorians in our community, who are using tools and technologies, these new mediums and channels to be able to reach people globally. It is possible today, it really is.

10. What do you see is your role in achieving this desire?

Aziza:

Providing accessibility to Montessori in marginalised communities, to the women and children who are not usually accounted for in these initiatives. For example, at the moment, the global Montessori workshops and Montessori schools are not accessible to marginalised communities, like refugees who live in remote areas and do not have access to a stable internet connection or electricity. Having worked with these communities for over a decade, my mission would be to provide access to Montessori to marginalised communities. Hopefully, I will be on the route to achieving that with the help of Montiplay and people like yourself.

Aziza's chosen poem:

RUMI

What will our children
do in the morning
if they do not see us fly?

A peek into the world of Aziza

Images: (Left) *Refugee Camp set up by UNHCR in Bekaa Valley, Lebanon* **(Right)** *Refugee children at the Jusoor center for literacy and education in Beirut, Lebanon 2015*

The Montessori Mission, by Charlotte Awdry

Images: From top, left to right
(1) *Layla, my daughter* **(2)** *Gold dervish 1 Painting by Rana Chalabi, Egypt.* **(3)** *Visiting refugee families in their home in Sabra Shteila.* **(4)** *Lebanon 2015*

Reflective practice

1. Journal

"Our language of communication at home has always been Arabic but I tended to switch to English when we were outside of our home. The first time I observed this about myself, I tried to evaluate why this was the case. Why do I attempt to speak a language in front of others and try to perfect the accent? Is it to show that I am equal or on par with the outside world? To not feel like a second-class citizen, the way I did growing up as a child in Europe, when I felt embarrassed speaking Arabic or maintaining our culture?"
Aziza Osman (2021)

Aziza speaks of the duality she felt as an Arab growing up in Europe, speaking Arabic at home and switching to English when she was outside of the home to avoid feeling othered.

With this in mind...

- Reflect upon a time in recent memory where you have changed your true self in order to fit in with a group.
- How did this lack of congruence within you present itself?
- And how did you feel when you became aware of it?

2. Embodiment

"With Montessori I believe that I have gained confidence in the way that I parent, it has given me the self-love that I needed to go on the parenting journey." **Aziza Osman (2021)**

Aziza describes how she has gained confidence during her parenting journey and has been taught so much about self-love and acceptance through her relationship with her daughter.

The Montessori Mission, by Charlotte Awdry

With this in mind:

- Take a moment to close your eyes and place one hand over your heart. Breathe deeply there, feel what self-acceptance, self-love and self-confidence might feel like in your body.
- In what ways do you embody self-love, self-confidence and acceptance?

3. Creativity

Think of a memory which brings to you feelings of freedom, fun and joy, a time when you felt comfortable to express your true self freely. If such a memory does not come easily, consider what it might be like to feel this way in the future.

Draw, paint, sculpt, compose, write or dance about the strong feelings that are evoked from imagining this version of yourself.

Share your thoughts...

I would love to hear your thoughts, so feel free to share them via any of the following ways to the Montessori Mission community:

- Email me sayhello@enrichingenvironments.com
- Tag me @enrichingenvironments and use the hashtag #montessorimission on Instagram & Facebook

Pilar Bewley

Born in Mexico and now living with her children and husband on the original land of the Kumeyaay people in the United States. Pilar is a former Montessori child, attending Scripps Montessori in San Diego, California.

A Montessori advocate, a mompreneur and homeschool mentor, Pilar holds AMI certifications for ages 3-12, a Master's degree in Montessori Education, Positive Discipline parent and classroom certifications, and the Orff Schulwerk I diploma. For over a decade, Pilar worked in Montessori classrooms and blogged extensively about Montessori in real life. She left the classroom to homeschool her two children at the end of 2018; and in May 2020, Pilar created MainlyMontessori.com to provide resources and support for homeschooling parents. Pilar has such a unique perspective to share, a wealth of classroom experience and three years' homeschool experience.

I love Pilar's work and have participated in her homeschooling hub retreat: an eight-week course with weekly zoom calls, videos, homework and downloads. Even though I am not currently a homeschooler, I found the resources within the hub and on the course to be of huge value. Pilar has also been a regular guest on my Instagram Live sessions, talking about the Elementary child, and in particular helping us to understand the intricacies of moving from the First Plane (0-6 years) to the Second Plane (6-12 years). She has been a huge support for me as a friend, as a colleague and as a Montessorian, helping me to navigate this new stage with my daughter, Olivia, and just life in general.

The Montessori Mission, by Charlotte Awdry

We begin the 10 Questions...

Pilar:

I love how we have connected across the oceans halfway around the world. This opportunity is just so dear to my heart, so I am very grateful.

1. What does Montessori mean to you?

Pilar:

It has meant a lot of things to me over the years. It is a way of knowing myself, understanding who I am, how I respond, and how I see the world. It is also a way of knowing my children and understanding the path that they are walking. We get so many conflicting messages from society as to what parents and children should be doing. Montessori gives me the freedom and trust to say: "What you need to know is already inside of you, and what your children need is already inside of them." That is what I think Dr. Montessori discovered when she was observing the children, and it is one of the reasons that she speaks about the Secret of Childhood. Children already have that inside them, and it will guide their development; it never ends, it builds on each stage of growth because children and adults are always growing and evolving.

Charlotte:

That is so true, it's a spiral; our knowledge begins and the same things come around every cycle, whether it is a year or six months, and we understand it on a deeper, richer level. Something like that happens with our own self-knowledge and our knowledge about our children. And, as you said, the gift Dr. Montessori gave us was telling us to access and trust our inner wisdom.

Pilar:

I think this spiral curriculum, where you are able to put the children back in touch with the same concepts, but at a more abstract and more complex level, is a micro-reflection of our greater experience as human beings, where we go back to the same experiences. We follow a path, but each time we are able to bring our prior experiences to it, and so we see it with new eyes, just like an older child will see the same topic with new eyes. The more we work with children and work on ourselves, the more we see ourselves with new eyes because we bring those experiences with us. It is very reflective of the human experience, and that is what I love about Montessori.

Charlotte:

We have a path to travel, and I think, as Montessori parents, it gives us that trust to allow our children to open in that way. As you said, there is so much pressure from what is going on outside, but hopefully Montessori gives us this gift of every time coming back to, "What does my child need at this moment?"

Pilar:

Absolutely. The trust that Montessori allows you to have in your child is really powerful. But also, the trust that Montessori allows you to have in yourself. One of my main missions is helping adults to trust themselves because most of us were not trusted when we were little. This was through no fault of our parents, they were also just victims of a system, but if we can be the cycle-breakers, that could be so powerful. Montessori allows us to be the cycle-breakers because we know that we are not alone, we are working with our child's inner development and we have a partner in this. When we start trusting that we are not alone, then we are better able to trust ourselves. When we see that our child has an inner drive, then we start understanding that we do too. We start understanding that we have an instinct and an awareness that we need to quiet all of those external voices. And then when we do, the truth of who we are, and that connection between us and the child becomes more evident. Montessori allows us to do that, it gives us a framework of how to do it.

Charlotte:

It comes back to connection every single time.

2. What was your first light bulb moment on your Montessori journey?

Pilar:

I would love to say that it was when I was a child, but to me Montessori was just what I knew, it wasn't anything transcendent in my childhood. I didn't know that other children went to schools where children weren't respected and where children with learning differences were treated like everybody else. To me, it was just normal. But what really convinced me that Montessori was the path was during my first observation. I arrived back to the Montessori world, not really even knowing why I was there; I was 30 and I had a successful wedding planning business. I was making a lot of money, but I wasn't feeling like I was contributing to the world in a way that I wanted to. As a Montessori child, you want to give back to the world, it is within you. So, I sat down to meditate and just put out this question: "What should I do with my life?" And a voice came to me and said, "You need to work with children." I knew I wanted to have children but I saw children, like most of the developed world, as loud, obnoxious, rude and messy. And, so, I questioned why I would want to work with children, and this voice would not leave me alone. I talked to my then fiancé, and he said, "You always talk about your childhood and Montessori, so why don't you start there?" The AMI Training Centre was across the street from his house, which was the first sign, so I went to talk to the Director, and it turns out, the Director was from Mexico City, and her daughter and I had gone to high school together. I was still running my business and joined the course, honestly not knowing why I was there. And when you are doing your training, you do observations, you sit down and watch the children working, and you try to see them with the eyes of a scientist, objectively without jumping to any conclusions. I was observing this little girl who was four, and she was sitting down working with a metal inset. When she was done, she stood up, put all of her materials on a tray and very carefully took the tray and returned all the materials to the shelf. I realise that all children are capable of doing this but when I saw her composure, poise and self-discipline, at the age of four, it blew me away.

It allowed me to see what children are truly capable of, how we misinterpret their behaviours and what little value we place on their development and potential.

That was my light bulb moment; and I am not going to say that it has been all puppies and unicorns because I had 30 years of conditioning that I had to work through, but I have never forgotten this child and the impact that she had on my life.

Charlotte:

Four-year-olds are so powerful, I see it with my four-year-old son Harry, that sense of order and precision, needing everything to be absolutely perfect in that way. You see the inner drive and there is something about four-year-olds that is magnetic to watch.

Pilar:

It is like they are coming into their own and realising their potential. Dr. Montessori said that in the first three years, the child is an unconscious creator and then around the age of three, they become a conscious worker. So, at the age of four, all of that is solidifying, and they are at the pinnacle of the First Plane. The Second Plane tendencies aren't coming in yet but the First Plane tendencies are so well-developed at that point. And I think that is what makes them so powerful, they have a drive to work and are so capable, they have this Absorbent Mind.

Charlotte:

He can do all the things that I can do, he's just a smaller person. He can cook a meal, he can put the washing out, he can do the ironing, he's in the workshop sawing pieces of wood and hammering, and he mended the hoover when it broke. He can do the things an adult can do but he is just miniature.

Pilar:

At four they are right in the middle of all the sensitive periods for the First Plane. It is this remarkable period of growth and with it comes a lot of frustration if they are not given the space and ability to express themselves; and that is where a lot of misconceptions lie.

Charlotte:

The impulse control isn't quite there yet, like with Harry, he is very physical, he will come and give you a bear hug and knock you to the ground, so it is really easy to misunderstand what is going on.

Pilar:

People have to know what to look for; you can't see something that you don't know is there, and that is where the education piece lies.

The humility has to be there on the part of the adult to say, "I don't know everything about this child in front of me and I want to learn, I want to be able to support them, and therefore I am going to educate myself on what they are truly capable of."

Once you do, it becomes so enjoyable to see a tendency for perfection, or a need to communicate. And so, when you know what you are looking at, you are much better able to understand those impulses that you are talking about.

3. In what ways does Montessori enrich the work that you do?

Pilar:

Oh, goodness, it is my whole life, I don't think that there is an area of my life that hasn't been touched by it. But in general, it has really allowed me to have a friendliness with error. I am a person that likes to create new things, I like to start projects and get out there and I don't know everything when I start. And Montessori allows me to have that beginner's mind of taking on new ventures, being okay with making mistakes, and honouring mistakes as opportunities for learning. One thing that Montessori has really done for me is rekindle my love of learning. I went to a traditional school when I was in the fourth grade because there were no Elementary schools in the city where I moved to. I always enjoyed school but I fell prey to the model of: "You have to learn this because it's on the test and because you need to get into college." Everything is an extrinsic goal, you learn for the sake of moving to the next stage, not just for the joy of learning. When I took my Elementary training in Italy, I rediscovered the joy of learning for its own sake. In my work with parents, I find that some parents are able to rediscover that when they are homeschooling. And I love that about Montessori, it really brings people back to the core of learning just for the joy of it. The last point that comes to mind with Montessori enriching all that I do is that we are planting seeds.

When you work with Elementary children, the idea is not that you are teaching them to memorise and regurgitate, what you are doing is scattering and broadcasting seeds of knowledge and culture. And you are trusting that they are going to take hold in the child's mind, and that the right ones, the ones that the child needs, are going to start to grow.

Sometimes that growth happens immediately, sometimes the growth happens into the adolescent years. But that is not for us to determine and I have found the same applies to my work with parents. When I first started sharing, recording and creating everything that I do, I was really concerned about whether or not the parents were going to understand what I was saying, whether it was going to make sense, and whether it was going to work for them. And I realised that, just like I cannot control what the children learn, I cannot control what the parents learn. And so, my approach has shifted towards broadcasting seeds, broadcasting my experience, the wisdom that the children have shared with me over the years, and paying it forward, and trusting that each parent is going to take what they need. It has worked really well and has released me from the pressure of being perfect. And going back to that friendliness with error, it has also allowed parents to take what resonates with them at that particular point in time and not feel pressured about understanding everything perfectly the first time.

Charlotte:
I love the seeds analogy and not having the need to check up on them but just trusting that we have planted them. We don't plant something in winter and then dig it out every two weeks to see what is going on—we just trust that in April or early May

something is going to happen. As you said from the beginning, it is all about trust: trusting that we are enough and trusting that our children are enough. We are all on this cosmic path and whatever is the right thing will reveal itself to us or to our child as long as we can get out of the way and trust whatever comes forth.

4. When was the first time a child taught you something about yourself that you weren't aware of?

Pilar:

I always thought that when I finished my Primary training, I would be prepared and ready to be a teacher. And my first year as a Primary Guide was the most tremendous kick in the butt. Those children, bless their hearts, had to deal with a brand new Guide, who had never even worked with children before, so it was such a learning journey for all of us.

When you are in a classroom, the children are reflecting back to you every single moment the things that you have to work on, if you are open to seeing it. But there was one incident that really broke me. I was working at a school where there was a lot of pressure placed on the teachers from the Director, parents and investors, to create a perfect Montessori environment. When there is pressure like that in a school, the teachers unconsciously deflect it towards the students, it is human nature, especially if you are a new Guide and don't have the spiritual grounding yet. The children are such pure and raw little spiritual beings, they bear the brunt of it, take it on, and have nobody to deflect it to. I had a-four-year-old student who showed me a drawing that she had made of the school. I looked at the drawing, expecting it to be flowers and sunshine, but it was a building with a child behind a barred window, and there was a bubble coming out of the window which said, "No, no, no, no, no." It broke my heart, because that one drawing reflected my approach of trying to create the classroom that I thought I had to have. But instead of going about it in a positive way and creating the conditions that would allow for a peaceful and joyful environment to happen, I was saying, "No, don't do this, don't do that, don't do the other." It had turned into a classroom of nos, and this child allowed me to see that through her drawing; it transformed everything inside of me. I apologised to her and to myself—I had to allow the guilt to come through and friendliness with error to come through, to really understand that we were not going to get to where we want to by saying no to everything, by removing everything that we don't want.

5. When was the last time a child taught you something about yourself that you weren't aware of?

Pilar:

My children are my guiding lights. My son has been an avid, voracious reader from the time he was five; and I was curious to know why my daughter, who is six, hadn't been gravitating towards books. The other day I was sitting at the dining room table, completely engrossed in a book; my daughter looked at me, walked over to her basket of beginner readers, pulled out her book, and came to sit beside me. That was the first time that she had done that.

I spend a lot of time on social media because that is where my business lies, I also use it for news and sometimes to escape. I think a lot of us do, we just tune out when the world becomes too burdensome. My daughter doesn't know that I am on social media and reading, she just sees me doing it. But she is learning from me and from what I do; she wants to be like me, and I need to be constantly aware of the messages that I am sending her through my behaviour. So, I have started putting my book on top of my cell phone when it is charging, so that when I go to get my cell phone I remember to pick up the book. These little changes can make a big difference.

6. When was the last time a child caught you out of integrity and questioned you on it?

Pilar:

My six year old is entering the sensitivity for morality in the Second Plane, and is fearless about questioning me, which I am really happy about. I think I was too strict and too intransigent with my first child. Poor first children, they always get the brunt of our mistakes! I am really happy to see that my second child is so outspoken. When she asked me to play with her, I would say, "Yes, but let me do this other thing first." She would get really irritated and say, "You always do something else first and you always make me wait, and that is not fair." So, I started asking myself, why am I doing this? At first I thought it was because I was so busy, but therapy has really allowed me to see that her request is a reminder to my wounded child that it actually exists. And that is the moment when that child also wants to be put first. When you are a parent, especially in a homeschooling setting, you are always putting other people's needs first. So, I have taken my daughter's requests as an opportunity to validate my inner child's need to be taken into account, to say, "It's okay, I see you, there will be time for you." It allows me to say yes, without any conditions, and allows me to stay more present because I can take care of the child that is within me. That has been a big gift, but it really took her getting angry and speaking out for me to see what was inside of me.

Charlotte:

That is so beautiful and though-provoking, thank you; I think it is going to resonate with a lot of people. In my own journey, Olivia drew my attention to when Harry would ask for something, I would go immediately, but if she asked for something, I would say, "Let me just do this first." I am still unpicking that but it is very, very interesting. As you said, when we can observe and then start to pay attention and take care of our inner child, then it changes everything. It changes our relationship with our children, and it changes the way we interact with the outside world.

7. How did you explain yourself when you were out of integrity?

Pilar:

When your child calls you out, and you have the fortitude to really dig inside and see what is going on, just a simple, "You are right, I am sorry." I think that modelling a different way of doing things and focusing on changing our actions in the long run is more powerful than empty words. I think that is the wonderful thing about having that connection and love with our child; when they are showing us these parts of ourselves, the love allows us to commit to working on it and not shoving it aside because it is uncomfortable.

8. What is your favourite Dr. Montessori quote at this moment in time?

Pilar:

My current favourite quote is: "The child's parents are not his makers but his guardians" [1]. It goes back to this idea that there is an inner guide and nature co-parenting with you and co-guiding the child. We are entrusted with taking care of this being that came through us, but is not ours. We didn't make the child consciously, they are a creation of nature or God, of the Universe or whatever you want to call it, and we are just entrusted to guard their development, and then eventually they are going to move on.

The Montessori Mission, by Charlotte Awdry

Charlotte: I love that, it is beautiful and reminds me of the Khalil Gibran poem, "Your children are not your children" that Barbara chose for the beginning of her chapter.

Pilar:

It aligns so well with the same idea: we don't make them, we are just here to take care of them and hopefully not mess them up.

Charlotte:

To guide them on their path.

Pilar:

Absolutely. We are just here to be models of what it's like to be an imperfectly perfect human being. We are just models of what it is like to go through life with its ups and downs, with its joys and sorrows. So, this idea that we have to be perfect or that we have to make them perfect is obviously destructive at its worst.

Charlotte:

It is really flawed. In Episode Four when I was speaking to Trisha Moquino from Cochiti Pueblo in New Mexico, she talked about this unattainable idea of perfection in colonial thinking. It is ludicrous pressure that we have in the western world to put a mask that we are perfect just for our ego.

Pilar:

It is so destructive and it really limits creativity.

9. What is your deepest desire for Montessori for the future?

Pilar:

I think it goes back to what we were talking about at the beginning. I would love for it to just be a birthright for children, parents, and adults in general, because we come into contact with children in so many different ways. So, even if you are not a parent, just understanding this new perspective on children can be transformative for all of society. I have always thought: what if it didn't have the name Montessori? The name defines it and I use it because that is how I know people will find it—but the name limits it, too, because of the way that Montessori is perceived. It is so limiting, it is perceived as materials and as these cute shelves with little themes and trinkets. With the name you limit it, but without the name, how do you define it? So, that is what I would love for Montessori to become.

I would love for Montessori to be normalised as a path of growth for adults and children, and as a way to respect children and empower adults as principles for living.

Montessori gave us the planes of development, but she could have gone further, and I think anybody who has moved through early adulthood and into their 30s, and 40s realises that we go through more stages.

Charlotte:

Early 40s, oh, my goodness! That was a wild ride, wasn't it?

Pilar:

Yes! And it has this same pattern as early childhood through to adolescence. So, wouldn't it be wonderful to continue that study of planes of development to help adults to understand themselves better using the same principles? The principles are universal and timeless, they follow the child through into adulthood. But how fascinating for people to be able to see themselves in these planes and to better understand themselves? That would be really fun. What is so powerful about Montessori is that the principles come from observation. There have been many educational theories that come from somebody's idea of how things should be and they are very honourable—they are people who wanted to change the world for the better and to help children. But to have principles that come from pure observation, we shouldn't even have to call it anything. All we need to do is help people see it in their children. Unfortunately, in our commercial society, everything has to have a label. Everything has to have a name for it to be considered valid and acceptable, and for people to embrace it. And that is what has kept the name Montessori attached to it, and again, that also limits it. So, I think just keep writing, speaking, and sharing, and as parents embrace these ideas, they will become more mainstream. We all want to better understand our children, we all want an approach that allows us to be more human.

Charlotte:

A more peaceful and harmonious world! No one can argue with that, because everyone wants it and this is the path to do it. I love how you said it is pure observation; it's not based on someone else's opinion, which is circling back to what we said at the beginning. Dr. Montessori's gift that she gave us was that everyone has the power to see this within their child and with everyone else's child. It is nothing more than observation. We don't need to do a course or for our child to go to a Montessori school—the child tells us everything we need to know, and that is what the gift is.

Pilar:

And you know what is really wild is that whole idea of normalisation. Dr. Montessori, in The Absorbent Mind, writes that normalisation was the most important result of her work. She didn't set out to normalise children—normalisation happened and she observed it. As she made little changes to the environment and to the preparation of the adults, all of that led to the normalisation of the children. And we are constantly taking the opposite approach. In schools, normalisation becomes an extrinsic goal, it is something to push the child towards, as opposed to a phenomenon that occurs when all the conditions are right. It is just like we try to manipulate everything in life, we try to manipulate birth, we try to manipulate health, we try to manipulate children. One of the things that I would love to see is for heads of schools, Guides, and parents to understand and see that this normalisation process is something that is reached—it is not something that is created or artificially forged.

Charlotte:

And I think when we read the text we can become confused about that when we are looking for signs of normalisation; we should just let our children be children. I have a client, her daughter is four and doesn't want to do activities with her at home, she just wants to play; so, I suggested she just let her play. And she said, I had transformed her view because she had been getting angry and frustrated because she wanted normalisation, when her daughter just wanted to play.

Pilar:

Normalisation is not constant, it's not solid, there are ebbs and flows. There are things that happen in a child's life that will shift them into a state of normalisation, or out of a state of normalisation—it goes back and forth. The same thing happens with the child; what we really ought to be doing is looking for signs of Sensitive Periods and Human Tendencies. Because when we guide and support these Sensitive Periods and Human Tendencies, the result becomes normalisation without us focusing on it. We are focusing on the end when we should be focusing on the conditions that will naturally lead the child towards that higher state of being.

Charlotte:

If we look for signs of normalisation then we are almost setting our child up to fail. It's a test, isn't it?

Pilar:

It is digging up the seeds to see if they are growing, and killing them.

10. What do you see is your role in achieving this desire?

Pilar:

What has really been speaking to me has been to lead through example, and by that I don't mean being the perfect shining example of Montessori. Quite the contrary,

> *I share my struggles and talk about how I work on myself and share some of my children's opportunities for growth, their own struggles and the things they are discovering. I really think this is the way to connect with the people who have a misperception that Montessori is a perfect and pristine method of teaching children.*

If they see a person that has been immersed in Montessori all of their life, and still has a messy kitchen, still gets angry and messes up the lesson, then maybe they can see that Montessori is for them. Being vulnerable and letting go of perfection and the image that social media wants you to have is what I strive for and I have found that it resonates with parents who are ready to do the work. That is my goal right now, to just be myself and help others and know that there are many ways to Montessori right there.

Charlotte:

That is so lovely Pilar, and that is what I see in what you share, you just show the magic and the ordinary because that is what daily life is like. The messy bits, the vulnerable bits and the bits where you get it wrong, and then there are these amazing moments as well, playing on the tyre swing and climbing trees. But it is all part of the realness and the rawness, and that is why it is such a value for parents because it resonates.

Pilar:

I never thought that I would work with parents like that. When I was working with children in the classroom my biggest struggle was working with parents. But now that I am working with parents without the children, it has been so fascinating to see them going through their own planes of development. Often times in the classroom children learn better from other children than they do from the adult, because the older child has just walked that path, so it is fresh, and approachable. That is how I see your role and my role as parents who are walking one step ahead, modelling and sharing with the parents who are ready.

The Montessori Mission, by Charlotte Awdry

Images: From top, left to right
(1) Wedding Scene in Tree of Life
Sculpture - By Damaso Ayala Jimenez-
Casa de Montejo-Merida-Mexico. **(2)**
Tree of Life with theme of handcrafts
by Oscar Soteno on display at the
Museum of Artes Populares in Mexico
City. **(3)** Pilar current homeschool coop
- November 2021. **(4 and 5)** Pilar 1983 in
her Montessori classroom.

Hombres Necios que Acusáis

by Señor Juana Inès de la Cruz, Mexico

In Spanish

Hombres necios que acusáis
a la mujer sin razón,
sin ver que sois la ocasión
de lo mismo que culpáis:

   si con ansia sin igual
solicitáis su desdén,
¿por qué quereis que obren bien
si las incitáis al mal?

   Combatís su resistencia
y luego, con gravedad,
decís que fue liviandad
lo que hizo la diligencia.

   Parecer quiere el denuedo
de vuestro parecer loco,
al niño que pone el coco
y luego le tiene miedo.

   Queréis, con presunción necia,
hallar a la que buscáis,
para pretendida, Thais,
y en la posesión, Lucrecia

   ¿Qué humor puede ser más raro
que el que, falto de consejo,
el mismo empaña el espejo
y siente que no esté claro?

   Con el favor y el desdén
tenéis condición igual,
quejándoos, si os tratan mal,
burlándoos, si os quieren bien.

   Opinión, ninguna gana:
pues la que más se recata,
si no os admite, es ingrata,
y si os admite, es liviana

   Siempre tan necios andáis
que, con desigual nivel,

a una culpáis por crüel
y a otra por fácil culpáis.

   ¿Pues cómo ha de estar templada
la que vuestro amor pretende,
si la que es ingrata, ofende,
y la que es fácil, enfada?

   Mas, entre el enfado y pena
que vuestro gusto refiere,
bien haya la que no os quiere
y quejaos en hora buena.

   Dan vuestras amantes penas
a sus libertades alas,
y después de hacerlas malas
las queréis hallar muy buenas.

   ¿Cuál mayor culpa ha tenido
en una pasión errada:
la que cae de rogada
o el que ruega de caído?

   ¿O cuál es más de culpar,
aunque cualquiera mal haga:
la que peca por la paga
o el que paga por pecar?

   Pues ¿para quée os espantáis
de la culpa que tenéis?
Queredlas cual las hacéis
o hacedlas cual las buscáis.

   Dejad de solicitar,
y después, con más razón,
acusaréis la afición
de la que os fuere a rogar.

   Bien con muchas armas fundo
que lidia vuestra arrogancia,
pues en promesa e instancia
juntáis diablo, carne y mundo.

English Translation

Silly, you men–so very adept
at wrongly faulting womankind,
not seeing you're alone to blame
for faults you plant in woman's mind.

After you've won by urgent plea
the right to tarnish her good name,
you still expect her to behave–
you, that coaxed her into shame.

You batter her resistance down
and then, all righteousness, proclaim
that feminine frivolity,
not your persistence, is to blame.

When it comes to bravely posturing,
your witlessness must take the prize:
you're the child that makes a bogeyman,
and then recoils in fear and cries.

Presumptuous beyond belief,
you'd have the woman you pursue
be Thais when you're courting her,
Lucretia once she falls to you.

For plain default of common sense,
could any action be so queer
as oneself to cloud the mirror,
then complain that it's not clear?

Whether you're favored or disdained,
nothing can leave you satisfied.
You whimper if you're turned away,
you sneer if you've been gratified.

With you, no woman can hope to score;
whichever way, she's bound to lose;
spurning you, she's ungrateful–
succumbing, you call her lewd.

Your folly is always the same:
you apply a single rule
to the one you accuse of looseness
and the one you brand as cruel.

What happy mean could there be
for the woman who catches your eye,
if, unresponsive, she offends, yet whose
complaisance you decry?

Still, whether it's torment or anger–
and both ways you've yourselves to blame
– God bless the woman who won't have
you, no matter how loud you complain.

It's your persistent entreaties
that change her from timid to bold.
Having made her thereby naughty,
you would have her good as gold.

So where does the greater guilt lie
for a passion that should not be: with the
man who pleads out of baseness
or the woman debased by his plea?

Or which is more to be blamed–
though both will have cause for chagrin:
the woman who sins for money
or the man who pays money to sin?

So why are you men all so stunned
at the thought you're all guilty alike?
Either like them for what you've made
them or make of them what you can like.

If you'd give up pursuing them, you'd
discover, without a doubt, you've a
stronger case to make against those who
seek you out.

I well know what powerful arms
you wield in pressing for evil: your
arrogance is allied with the world, the
flesh, and the devil!

Reflective practice

1. Journal

Pilar describes how her daughter would become frustrated when she asked her to play with her and she would say, "Yes. But let me do this other thing first." Her daughter told her that she did not think this was fair because she always had to wait.
With this in mind, journal upon the following...

- How often do we allow ourselves to prioritise being with our children over the many other household tasks we have to do?
- What times during the day (even if it is just 15 minutes) can we be there with our child, respond to their call, connect straight away to read or play?
- What part of us and our inner child needs to feel seen before we can do this naturally and without resentment?

2. Embodiment

"The trust that Montessori allows you to have in your child is really powerful. But also, the trust that Montessori allows you to have in yourself. One of my main missions is helping adults trust themselves because most of us were not trusted when we were little."
Pilar Bewley (2021)

Pilar speaks passionately about learning to trust ourselves, and with this in mind, for our embodiment practice, I invite you to consider the following:

- What sensations do you feel in your body when you really trust yourself and trust a decision you are making (big or small)?
- What are the messages that your body gives you to let you know that you are in alignment with what is right for you?
- Feel into these feelings of self-trust so you can call upon them at a later time.

Bring this practice of listening to your body's messages into your daily life, so that you and your children can begin to embody trusting your body's wisdom.

3. Creativity

"Montessori allows me to have that beginner's mind of taking on new ventures, being okay with making mistakes, and honouring mistakes as opportunities for learning. One thing that Montessori has really done for me is rekindle my love of learning."
Pilar Bewley (2021)

Let us rekindle our love of learning by experiencing some part of our world as a "beginner" again. I invite you to learn something new, with your child, just for fun! The activity you choose should be child-led, but of course will depend on the age of your child. Here are a few ideas, but I know that yours will be alot more creative than mine!

- For a baby: Lie on the floor next to them and as you observe them, mirror their movements, their kicks, stretches and yawns. When they are rolling or crawling, do the same, follow them, be in their world. Slow down enough so that you can learn to experience the world as they do.
- For a toddler: Get in the kitchen and cook something together, something that they like but that you have never cooked before with them.
- For a preschooler: Choose something that your child is interested in but you are not (for example, insects or reptiles). Allow yourself to be challenged by their choice of interest to pursue together.
- For an Elementary and Adolescent child: Step into their world, learn a new skill associated with their age group, like skateboarding, reading and writing comics, street dance or rapping—an activity that allows you to see more of the world through their eyes.

This activity enables us to put aside our preferences and learn about something that we do not enjoy. A recent example in my own journey, which might be helpful, was when my daughter Olivia developed a strong interest in weapons at around the age 6. It seemed so macabre to me and contrary to my vision of a more peaceful and harmonious world, through Montessori. However, I did my best to lean into her interest and found a really interesting book about weapons through the ages to satisfy her curiosity and to develop her knowledge. The more we learned about how weapons evolved, the more fascinated we became. And through these discoveries she reached her own conclusion that weapons can be destructive. I didn't need to give any moral lessons, Olivia understood what she needed to at that time.

Share your thoughts with me and the community...
Email me at <u>sayhello@enrichingenvironments.com.</u> Join me on Instagram & Facebook @enrichingenvironments and use #montessorimission

CHAPTER 8

Tatenda Blessing Muchiriri

Born and raised in Zimbabwe and now residing in Denver, United States, on the original land of the Southern Ute Indian Tribe and Ute Mountain Ute Tribe.

Tatenda Blessing Muchiriri is a powerful Afro Montessori advocate and currently serves as a board member for the Colorado Montessori Association. He first discovered Montessori by chance whilst travelling in Beijing, China, sending him on a trajectory that completely changed his life. He spent several years in Beijing before moving to the U.S. in 2014, where his love of Montessori led him to study and become certified in Montessori from birth to six years old at the American Montessori Society (AMS). Tatenda also has an Undergraduate degree in Liberal Arts and is pursuing a Master's in International Education Administration. He was privileged to be part of the AMS Emerging Leaders Fellowship 2018, Moonshot EdVentures 2020 and the Iterative Space Fellowship 2021, and Moon and Stars Association. He is also a regular guest speaker for the Montessori Education Centre of the Rockies and City Garden Montessori Institute. He is currently working on some incredible NGO projects, and is in the process of developing a passion project called Montessori on Wheels, which aims to transform the way that Montessori education can be delivered outside the traditional school building, and making it more accessible to Black, Brown and Indigenous communities. Tatenda is a lifelong learner in Afro-Indigenous educational pedagogies and is a leading light for Afro Montessori.

We begin the 10 Questions...

Tatenda:

Thank you so much. I am so humbled that you were able to connect and make time to share my experiences and insights.

Charlotte:

I think we need to hear the Beijing story because it is so awesome. Would you mind just talking us through how Montessori gave you this big blast from the universe that this was your path?

Tatenda:

I was actually thinking about it today, as I was preparing myself to be in this space with you, reflecting back to 2009 in Beijing. I was there for a film festival and, by chance, I was invited to audit a Montessori class. A person I had met at the festival had seen the work I had done in Zimbabwe with young children, in education, health, well-being and wellness, and he thought that I might have a unique perspective on education and young children. I had no idea what Montessori was then, so this was something very strange to me. I was just a boy from Zimbabwe, in China, trying to learn one or two words in Chinese to be able to communicate. And here I was being invited to a school to audit something that I had never heard about. So, I sat there for two hours in the morning, observing a Montessori classroom. I was so surprised; growing up in Zimbabwe, I went through the strict British apartheid education system, sitting at a desk and looking at the teacher at the blackboard. And here I was in Beijing where I could barely see the teacher in the classroom. These young children were just busy doing different work and rarely asking the teacher for help. And I don't know... something just felt strange, there were a lot of surprises in those two hours. I vividly remember one thing that was so different, but it was a reminder of how I grew up in Zimbabwe with my five big brothers, friends and neighbours where everything felt organic. And I was just convinced that this might be what I was searching for. So, I said yes to learning more about Montessori. I remember calling my mom, saying that I think I might have found a job in teaching and she said, "Go for it. I have always known you to be a teacher," which, again, was strange and surprising to me that she thought that I could teach. So, that is how I discovered Montessori with that uniqueness of being in Beijing, being invited and everything aligning with who I was, being exposed to something I had grown up with but it did not have a name.

Charlotte:

I think that is the best Montessori discovery story ever.

Tatenda:

I am still surprised with how I found myself in a Montessori classroom and I am more empowered by that experience.

Charlotte:

That is so true; empowerment changes us so much. Nusaibah, from Rumi Montessori said that it helps us to become more of the person we want to be and that really stuck with me, it really resonates. But also, But also, as a twenty year old, that is amazing that you felt that flash of inspiration. Twenty is quite young to realise that this is what you wanted to do and forging ahead with it.

Tatenda:

It gave me a clear definition of what empowerment is; it is something that is in us, that light and power that we have. And when I experienced something that was able to ignite what I already had, this power that I didn't know was within me, that moment, was just a game changer for me. It gave meaning to what I wanted to do with my life and how I thought about education. Montessori ignited that fire in me, like "Hey, you have this, this is it." Through that observation in Beijing, I was able to see myself.

Charlotte:

Wow! That is incredible. I feel really emotional hearing you speak, I haven't even asked the first question and I am crying already.

Tatenda:

I know, Montessori does that to us all.

1. What does Montessori mean to you?

Tatenda:

I think it means potential for what education can be. If done well, we can change the way we think about how children should learn and how we should facilitate environments of learning for children. It has the potential to change the way we think about families as partners more than just engaging them in our ways of teaching through a Montessori method.

With Montessori, I have experienced a way of thinking about how to partner with parents and affirming them as the child's first teacher; they have wisdom and know how their child learns. And being able to then take that and hold that sacred as we guide with what we know, through a Montessori method of how they learn.

The Montessori Mission, by Charlotte Awdry

It also has the potential, if done well, to honour communities and cultures. In Beijing, I saw it done in a way that was culturally relevant to Beijing. And being from Zimbabwe, I saw ways in which I was honoured and my childhood was in front of me.

Charlotte:

The parents have their inner wisdom, and we must hold that sacred whilst we guide their children; I love that.

Tatenda:

We don't really think about parents as being very knowledgeable about their child, because we think that we have been trained, and so we know. Which is not true because we are trained to have the language, framework and resources to be able to engage and partner with the parents. So, I like that it has that potential for us to welcome the parents, as we welcome the children as well.

Charlotte:

It feels as if that has been a huge shift in the past 10 years, it has become more about parent enrichment. I trained in 2011 MCI, in London, and at the beginning of my Montessori journey, there wasn't much, as you said, of the sacredness. But now, it feels that everything is ensuring this continuity, this congruence between the home and the classroom environment, so that we can work together as collaborators with the parents and the families as well as we do with the children. Do you feel in your experience that there has been a shift as well?

Tatenda:

Absolutely, I think there has been a shift. Even in my own training, which was very heavy on materials and giving lessons, but not so much about partnering with the parents or the knowledge of the child through the parents' experiences. I have seen the shift and can speak more about my experience in the United States where there has been a move to look at education through a racial lens or a gender lens. If we are able to serve the child, we really have to have a healthy relationship with the parents.

Charlotte:

It is really exciting and really positive. Going back to what you said about Beijing, you said that you felt that it was culturally relevant and they were sensitive to your culture as well. There is a brilliant quote from that great film, Inside Montessori, (Quiet Island Films, 2019) that children need a mirror and a window in the classroom and that resonates so deeply. It is so beautiful that you felt honoured and respected but you also felt that the children's culture was honoured and respected and revered as well. That is true Montessori, isn't it?

Tatenda:

I think being able to have the children experience this richness of who they are; it is visible in the environment, and the adults who are in the environment also feel a very strong sense of being seen and honoured, because we forget adults in many spaces. It is all about, "We have to save the children, we have to be able to guide the learning," but what about the adults who are also doing the work? Have they been affirmed? Are they being seen? Do they see themselves as well in this learning? So, my encounter with Montessori in Beijing was magical in a very spiritual way; everything in that moment felt like the Montessori light was shining in front of me.

Charlotte:

That is so powerful. When we were preparing for our chat, you said that the feeling, legacy and values of Montessori are what is really important, not just the name. And we must be careful that we are staying true to her values and her vision, not just paying lip service to the name. That's a challenge, isn't it?

Tatenda:

Indeed, it is. We are talking about the aware adults in Montessori; I think it takes the awareness of an adult who is really aware of who Maria Montessori was, more than the stories we are told or we read, but what brought her to what we now call Montessori? And then trying to live in some of those principles and question some of those so that we can do better.

2. What was your first light bulb moment on your Montessori path?

Tatenda:

It was Beijing, and to be more specific, it was the level of independence and freedom that was very vivid in that classroom. That day, I thought of myself back in Zimbabwe, just being outside with my friends and my brothers, living so free, running around, climbing trees, playing in the dirt and having freedom. That changed everything about how I thought about education. Maybe it is about independence, are they able to do things that we want them to learn? And also just thinking about what they want to learn, and guiding them. I think that independence and freedom was a game changer for me in the way we think about education; children will learn if they are independent, if they are able to do what they are supposed to do or what they want to do and knowing that they can do that.

Charlotte:

As adults, it takes such a deep level of trust, to trust ourselves and then trust the child. As you said, we must guide them to learn what they want to learn, and then know that once we have their trust, and we have helped them with their needs, then we can guide them if there is something else that has to be learned at that time. But it has to be them that that is the priority, not our agenda. It has to be their agenda and it is so hard as an educator, as a parent, even with training, it is really hard.

Tatenda:

Our definition of education is having somebody teach you things that you don't know that you need to know. I listened to your podcast with Barbara Isaacs when you were talking about the inner teacher within us. The child has an inner teacher, they know what they want to learn, and we can provide an environment where they can learn.

Charlotte:

Trust is a big one, and if we weren't trusted in childhood ourselves then that is a really big deal for us as adults. It's really interesting that you have spoken so much of that sense of freedom in your childhood, because when I spoke to Prudence at MomaHill Montessori in Lagos, she said the same. Her childhood consisted of outside freedom with her brother and sisters; a big family, lots of friends, and everyone doing their own thing. If they needed anything, they would come back home, grab it, and then go out again. In Western society, I feel we have lost that for our children, the freedom to go out because of fears, because the world is busy, because we are all working so much harder. We don't have the time to let our children go and play for three hours outside because there isn't the time. So, that sense of freedom that you speak of from your childhood, how can we give that back in modern Western society? And it has to be within the classroom, because that is where children have to be. So, how can we give them more freedom within the classroom that allows them to do what they need to do?

Tatenda:

It will take a lot of work, because some of it has to do with trust. Do we trust that they can just go outside and be able to take care of themselves? Think of my cultural shock when I moved to the United States and interacted with Western culture, just the amount of things that were considered risky, dangerous, or not safe for young children. I was like, "Oh my, that's my whole childhood." If you say that they cannot do this, they cannot even have access to doing this, then they won't be able to learn how to do it. So, I think being able to trust that it is safe outside.

I had a friend who would tell me that there is a reason why they are called toddlers, they toddle, they fall, they do all these things, but they are not going to break.

There are some limits but we are hands on to the extent that we sometimes hinder some of that adventure and exploration for our children, some of that muscle growth that they really need to climb trees and run around.

I think Western cultures need to learn from Indigenous cultures, they really need to do some deep listening and be willing to learn that we need to trust.

Charlotte:

I think there is a bigger question of trust in society, people have been let down by governments and organisations; there is a lack of trust. We feel like we can't trust anyone, because big companies aren't looking after us, they are looking after their profits, and governments aren't supporting us, or the police. We have got to find it within but then that is another whole spiritual growth, isn't it?

Tatenda:

It is so strange that we don't trust the system, we know that the system has failed us. I was very shocked to realise how education has been outsourced here and pretty much everywhere. We trust the schools to get our child to high school and to university. I think parents have to reclaim their children, so that they can own their experiences and learn with their children and have a partnership with teachers on how to create spaces and environments that are fully invested in how children should learn.

Charlotte:

The teacher training itself, the way that a teacher is taught in the mainstream system or even in the Montessori system, how they are taught to teach, that the child is a bucket to be filled. So, when they are coming from that, it is understandable that the teachers don't have the skills that they need to support children, because they are not even trained in a way that helps them to.

3. In what ways does Montessori enrich the work that you do?

Tatenda:

The work that I do is rethinking education in ways that it works for Black children, Black families, and African immigrants. I have tried to stay within my own experience, so that I can really understand it from where it comes from, where I am, and who I am, and people who might have the same experiences or shared experiences. With Montessori, I think it has, in itself, some of the ways which are very much aligned culturally to how we think about young children and how they should learn. And it gives me a framework of when I then talk to my Black families and I just tell them, "Hey, look, this is the story of our people, when we are doing Montessori, this is us. This is the thing that we were doing pre-colonisation, before the White settlers came."

The Montessori Mission, by Charlotte Awdry

Our forefathers, our grandfathers, our people, this is how they knew that children would learn if their bodies were moving, if their hands were having a sensory experience with objects. I think Montessori has really given me those insights that it can really be for anyone, and everyone if it is relevant to who they are and their lived experiences.

Charlotte:

As you said, wisdom has been there for thousands of years and we have made it super complicated when it doesn't need to be. You said that everything starts with movement, and I heard a great lecture all about how movement is the start of all cognition. Unless there is movement in the first five to six years, then the pathways haven't been laid for the high levels of the brain in order for cognition and the academic learning to come later on. As you said, it was instinctively known that children need to move and explore and do scary things when they are little, fall out of trees and break their arms, all of those things. It is so scary as a parent, but it is part of it; no one wants their child to bash their head but it is such a learning process for children to be able to understand their limits. But, I think, for Western parents, it is really hard to let go.

Tatenda:

This is very interesting to me, because I believe that they will not do anything that they are not ready to do. As a teacher, I don't help my children in the playground when they have to climb a structure; if they cannot do it themselves, I am not going to help them. Once they have the muscles built for it, they will do it. But if they are not there yet, and somebody has helped them to the top, that is when it is dangerous because they can't get back down, and when they try, they fall.

Talking about movement makes me think about a light bulb moment in Montessori when I took my infant and toddler training in Denver, Colorado. One of our instructors came to talk about movement, and she talked so much about natural birth, how the movements are very well coordinated and the baby is able to push themselves into the world. I was a premature baby, born via c-section, so I had to learn some of those movements and have my muscles aligned. This just speaks to the importance of movement, it is linked to how young children should learn.

Charlotte:

That is so interesting. I did an introductory Assistant to Infancy training course just outside Cape Town in Stellenbosch when I was pregnant with my daughter, Olivia. She was born via caesarean, and I was so mindful that I needed to facilitate her movement. I tried to do everything I knew from my training to make sure that I could support her in the best way, and she is now a super strong seven year old. So, I think we got the movement right; I don't know about anything else but she is really good at climbing trees now.

4. When was the first time a child taught you something about yourself that you weren't aware of?

Tatenda:

One of my all-time favourites is a funny story but it is also very rich when I think of the interaction that I had with one of the kids in my classroom, here in Denver. This was with an almost three year old and she had been learning how to use the bathroom. Western cultures tend not to potty train quickly, and then worry when it is supposed to happen, or when the school needs it to happen. I was very gentle, easy and trusted the process that it was going to happen.

One day, we were outside in the playground when she ran inside to use the bathroom; she came back and was like, "Hey, Mr. Tate!" At that time they used to call me Tate, not Tatenda. "Hey, Mr. Tate, I pooped for you!" It was during pickup time, so parents were there to pick up their kids, and there were kids in the playground; and she was so proud that she had pooped for me. I couldn't help but laugh. How many times do you hear somebody say that they have done this for you? It really gave me an insight into some of the work that I do that I may be not aware of, like, the role as teachers that we play because sometimes we don't know if they really remember us when they go home, or remember the work that we do. I knew then that I had so much to do as a teacher, more than just teaching.

Again, I think we get lost in teaching but we also aid and facilitate some of those social, physical growths that they need. It was a changing moment for me, the way that I think about toilet awareness and I now partner with parents and children to help them towards that independence. And it changed the way I think of myself and the way I think of myself as a teacher.

Charlotte:

I love that. The materials are such a tiny part, what we give them in self-confidence, body autonomy and body awareness is amazing.

5. When was the last time a child taught you something about yourself that you weren't aware of?

Tatenda:

When I came to the United States, I used to go by Tate, I thought it was cool, it was easy, short and neat. At the office, my name was Tate, so the kids called me Mr. Tate; I didn't introduce myself as Tatenda to the children in my classroom. One day a child came to me and said, "You are Tatenda, you are my African teacher." So, there were two things; she could say my name Tatenda which made me think, "Wow! Why am I not teaching them to say Tatenda? They can say Tatenda." And she also said that I was her African teacher, which brought me back again to ask, "Who am I as a teacher?" I had completed my infant and toddler training and my three to six training to become a Montessori teacher in the U.S. and I thought of myself just as a teacher who was trained in Montessori, and not about myself as an African.

Charlotte:

Honouring yourself and honouring your own cultural heritage.

Tatenda:

Yeah. It brought me back to so many things that I had been doing wrong. I remember during the month of February I was asked to talk about Nelson Mandela and Martin Luther King:

I was so proud to be able to share these stories with the kids but would forget that I am that Black person that they interact with every day. They need to hear my story, they need to learn about my family and the very beautiful stories that I can share with them. It really made me own my Zimbabwean identity and show up as an African Montessori teacher who is sharing the story of Montessori through my experiences.

Charlotte:

That is really powerful. As you said at the beginning, children need this mirror, they need to see people like them. And they need to see their Guide honouring their cultural heritage regardless of where they are from. They need us to be authentic, the most authentic we can be because that gives them permission to be authentic. They know if we are being incongruent, they can sniff it out; there is nothing like a young child to sniff out inauthenticity.

Tatenda:

They know!

Charlotte:

It is really interesting, they just shine a light on where we need to grow. Aziza Osman from Chapter 6 of this series is a powerful voice for Montessori here in the Arab world, and she describes a moment of realisation when she would speak Arabic at home with her daughter but switch to English when she was outside. She said that took her back to her childhood growing up in the Netherlands when she felt ashamed of being an Arab and was not able to celebrate her culture. She realised that she was now transferring that to her young daughter, of not honouring her heritage and pride in being an Arab.

Tatenda:

I can relate to that. Being an immigrant and a person who has lived in different parts of the world, in different cultures, you tend to hide some parts of yourself, for the fear of being identified as not somebody from that particular place. I remember when I was an assistant teacher not wanting to talk, because I knew that if I started talking, they would think I sounded different and know that I wasn't from there. And so, I resorted to being quiet and did not interact with the parents or with the children.

It took me reflecting on myself and how I wanted to show up and honour myself, that it was a gift for them to hear English spoken in a different accent.

To know that they are training themselves to listen and communicate with everyone, that people from around the world speak English in different accents. I give them the gift of being that teacher who has a different accent from their mom or whoever they interact with.

6. When was the last time a child caught you out of integrity and questioned you on it?

Tatenda:

It was a funny one; I always think anything with young children is always funny, they have a way to make it not too serious by just being young kids, it is adorable. It was in the first four weeks of school, so we were still trying to identify things in the environment and naming the work that we have on the shelves. We had our first birthday celebration and I had the globe. I was telling them that it is often called the Earth, because I wanted to teach them the idea of the Earth going around the sun as we were celebrating the birthday. But when we did the tour I had identified it as a globe, and this little boy said, "Oh, no. That is a globe." And I said, "Yeah. You are right." It made me think about the idea of being consistent. At that moment, I had not yet introduced to them the idea that the Earth goes around the sun, so it wasn't necessary for me to teach that lesson. The idea of Earth as a globe was not yet something that they could comprehend; so, it just made me think about consistency in the way that I teach.

Charlotte:

That is a really good example. It is meeting the child where they are, all the time.

7. How did you explain yourself when you were out of integrity?

Charlotte:

What did you say to the little boy, did you backtrack or did it flow naturally after that?

Tatenda:

In that moment I was able to recognise that he was right but I had to do some self-check on myself after that event and I questioned myself a lot, like, should I even celebrate a birthday when I haven't yet introduced the idea of the Earth?

Charlotte:

That's an interesting question.

Tatenda:

We normally introduce the globe when we are trying to introduce the continents and don't do that in the first four weeks of school, and yet we have some little ones who turned three in October who needed to be celebrated. I was able to acknowledge to the child that he was right, and as we were celebrating our friend's birthday, we were going to use this to represent the Earth.

8. What is your favourite Dr. Montessori quote, right now?

Tatenda:

I really like when she talks about the diversity of the Earth and how we should expose or give that to the child, so that they can really relish in that richness. I just love that that is our work, if we are able to start from whatever we introduce to them as being diverse so that they understand the idea of diversity and difference, before we introduce other bigger questions, or things that they need to learn.

Charlotte:

As you said, if we teach it as a whole from the beginning, the wholeness of the world and the different cultures within it, we don't have to do any unpicking later on.

Tatenda:

I have always been the first African male teacher at a school working with toddlers or infants; it is something that is unique when it shouldn't be unique. Why are we surprised that there is a man working with young children? We don't intentionally prepare environments where we expose our children to people who identify differently, be it male or female, transgender or gay. These are role models, teachers, adults, these are the people who were in my early foundation for my learning.

Charlotte:

It is going to take time to redress this balance through inspirational models like yourself, when you talk about giving children real experiences that they can relate to with people who are doing inspiring things in the world. You are here, you are going to make such a difference in the lives of children you work with, which is beautiful.

9. What is your deepest desire for Montessori in the future?

Tatenda:

I wish we could have a global way of thinking about Montessori, so that, again, it is not just thought of as Western or Eurocentric. One thing that I did last year, during the pandemic when people were baking bread, and doing all these recipes, I had time to connect with mainly immigrant families just to ask about their experiences with education in the United States and in their countries of birth, and their hopes for their children's education. I just tried to understand if they even knew what Montessori is.

We share Montessori in a very Eurocentric, Western way instead of including our Black and Brown families, Asian families or people who are not White. So, I really wish that Montessori could be interpreted and shared in a very diverse global way, so that we are not leaving others outside of that story, and outside of that education method.

So, my hope is that we will look at this as a framework that we were given to see what can be possible if education is done well, if children learn well using their body, if they learn using their senses, if we honour their love of learning. And there isn't anything Eurocentric in that. I was reading about when Montessori came to the United States and how they made it American, like they always do. Just as a way to commercialise it and make it appealing to affluent people, when it is something that should be accessible to every family and every child.

Charlotte:

You are right, inclusivity.

10. What do you see is your role in achieving this desire?

Tatenda:

I think being able to honour myself, my people, and reclaiming that for us. By us, I mean Black people, that this is ours too. I have a role to share this, to honour the spirit and my people who allow me to have the time to do this, to follow my dream, my passion to get trained and bring that back to them. I was the one to gain access to it, now here it is, so that we can all have access to Montessori education. It is more than being an advocate, it is really bringing it back. For those who read the Bible and go to church, after Jesus shared the parables with his disciples, they were told to go and share that with the world. So, I feel like one of those disciples in Montessori, I have had the privilege to gain access to it, and can now go back and share that with my community, people and family.

Charlotte:

That is beautiful; going back and doing that at a grassroots level. That is social change, isn't it? As you said, it's a gift, you being one of these disciples and then taking it back to Zimbabwe. But as you said, all the wisdom is there. That is what is so amazing, the wisdom of the way that you were raised, the way people are raised in traditional cultures. You know that the wisdom is there, and it is integrating it into the old, strict British school system. I guess Montessori is that bridge between the wisdom of traditional culture and your cultural heritage, with the old school system.

Talenda:

I believe that. People back home could use other ways of thinking about education, how their children should be educated, so that they just don't think that they have to pass that test to be able to proceed to Secondary school, then high school and college; when sometimes they might be gifted in ways that we don't know because they haven't been provided with the right environment. They have never had an adult who is so interested in who they are personally before thinking if they can write, or do addition. I really think that that is the work, to bring it back as an alternative to how we are taught to send our kids to school and expect them to excel in life.

Last year I was working to open a micro school here in Denver, through the Wildflower Schools Foundation. I was doing a fellowship through Moonshot Ventures, which allowed me time to work with Black, Brown, immigrant and refugee families in the community, to find out about their experiences with education and their awareness of Montessori education. I learnt that, as Montessorians and education entrepreneurs, we often expect parents to enrol their kids in school. We share information with the hope that they will enrol in the school in that neighbourhood. In many situations we don't really think about access in terms of transportation and being able to afford the tuition that most Montessori schools charge. When we think about extending Montessori to Black and Brown communities, we often think about it in terms of scholarships, but sometimes they really can't even afford those. Both in terms of paying for it or having their Black child be the only scholarship kid in a classroom of White kids who have different life experiences.

So, I thought of a program, called Montessori on Wheels, that will bring Montessori to them, to their homes, to their communities, to their churches, to their neighbourhood. Literally getting a bus and driving to their communities with the materials, so that they can get that exposure, and also to collaborate with the parent to think about what they have at home that can help the child to develop.

The program is still in its infant stage but we are building the team, and we have the bus! And I am excited to take the bus to the communities and have the kids come in and have fun with it. And then collaborate with the parents and really honour them as their child's first teacher, and think about ways in which we can honour what they know about their child. I want to take it back to Zimbabwe, move to the other side of the world where we hope to learn from Indigenous people and see if there are ways in which we can bring some of that back to our BIPOC communities here, so that they can become enriched in the ways we think about learning.

Charlotte:
I love it, Montessori on Wheels! It is such an interesting and beautiful project. Removing the privilege of people having to live in a certain neighbourhood or be in a certain income bracket to be able to get to a school, actually shifting that completely and going to people that need it is hugely powerful.

Talenda:
And not just thinking that schools are just buildings where they have to go to, home can also be a school. We are also deconstructing the idea of the school bus; the bus usually takes kids from home and to a school but in this case, it is coming to them and school is on the bus. I think there is so much deconstruction and decolonisation and honouring the parents as they realise that they do this naturally. What we do in Montessori is just that we have these materials helping us to do what they do at home naturally.

Charlotte:
What a vision! Thank you so much for sharing.

The Montessori Mission, by Charlotte Awdry

A peek into the world of Tatenda

Images: From top, left to right

(1) Africa, Mother with a child on her back – Beautiful art by my dear friend Kenneth Magwada, 15 years ago. At the heart of Africa, the cradle of mankind is the strength, love and wisdom of all the mothers. I carry that respect for my mother and all women as I seek to tap into their intuition and better the Montessori method of guiding children learning and development.

(2 onwards) Early photographs of me in Bejing, China where I discovered Montessori., and then moving into the US where I dived deep in the certification and learning from my greatest mentor Dr. Merrie B. King

Shava Museyamwa Totem

ORIGINAL LANGUAGE, SHONA

Shava Museyamwa
Maita Shava,
Mhofu yomukono, Ziwewera,
VokwaMutekedza, vakatekedzana paJanga,
Vakapihwa vakadzi munyika yavaNjanja.
Maita nhuka, Shava yangu yiyi,
Hekani Mutekedza, vari uHera Mukonde,
Zvaitwa Mhukahuru, vemiswe inochenga miviri,
Zienda netyaka, mutunhu une mago,
Vanovangira vashura vhu, kutsivira mutumbi,
Chidavarume, vanovhimwa navanonyanga,
Vakakamonera vakadzi dzenhema,
Vanomonera vakadzi dzamangondi,
Vanochemera wavatanga,
Vanemisodzi isodonha pasi,
Kuti yadonha yoda nhevedzo yaro romunhu ropa.
Tinotenda vari Matenhere,
Vari pazvikomo zveMbwenya.
Maita veTsambo chena, Mhofu yomukono,
Kuyambuka rwizi mvura yakwira makomo.
Totenda voMuchimbare, veGuruuswa,
Vanenzanga chena kunge mwedzi wejenachena,
Maita Museyamwa, Nhuka yangu yiyi,
Kuziva zvenyu vaShava Mukonde, vari Gombe.
Zvaonekwa vahombarume, zvaitwa Mbiru,
Aiwa, zvaonekwa Sarirambi, zvaitwa Nyashanu.

ENGLISH TRANSLATION

Thank you Shava
The Great Eland bull, The Runaway
Thank you very much The-one-who-carries heavy-loads
Those who challenged each other at Janga
Those who were given wives in the country of the Njanja people
Thank you my dear Mutekedza, those in uHera Mukonde
It has been done Great Animal, thosewith tails that are intimate with body

One with sounding feet, one who comb of wasps
Those who chase those who portend death, as compensation for a corpse
One-who-likes-men, hunted only by those who do so with caution
Those who do not wrap women with lies
Those who embrace and bend women

Those who yearn for the original one
Those with tears that are too sacred fall to the ground
But if they fall, they must be accompanied with human blood
We are so thankful those in Matenhere
Those who lie in the hills of Mbwenya
Thank you those of White Bangles, Great Eland Bull
Crossing the river after the waters have ascended the mountains
We are so thankful those in Muchimbare, those of Guruuswa
Those with white settlements that resemble the whiteness of the full moon
It is your custom to be kind, Shava Mukonde, those in Gombe
Your kindness has been seen great hunter, it has been done Mbiru
No, your kindness has been seen, Sarirambi, it has been done Nyashanu

Reflective practice

1. Journal

"So, I sat there for two hours in the morning, observing a Montessori classroom. I was so surprised; growing up in Zimbabwe, I went through the strict British apartheid education system, sitting at a desk and looking at the teacher at the blackboard. And here I was in Beijing where I could barely see the teacher in the classroom. These young children were just busy doing different work and rarely asking the teacher for help. And I don't know… something just felt strange, there were a lot of surprises in those two hours. I vividly remember one thing that was so different but it was a reminder of how I grew up in Zimbabwe with my five big brothers, friends and neighbours where everything felt organic. And I was just convinced that this might be what I was searching for."
Tatenda Blessing Muchiriri (2021)

- Reflect upon the 'flashes of inspiration' in your life that you feel have changed the course of your life, or have given you a deeper insight into who you want to be.

2. Embodiment

"With Montessori, I have experienced a way of thinking about how to partner with parents and affirming that sacredness as the child's first teacher; they do have wisdom and know how their child learns." **Tatenda Blessing Muchiriri (2021)**

- How does it feel in your body to honour the sacredness of you being your child's first teacher? Do you give yourself the credit you deserve for going into the 'toughest job you'll ever do' with little or no training at all?

Take a moment to feel the depth and breadth of the inner courage, wisdom and insight you have accessed since becoming a parent (whether your child is a newborn or an adult!).

3. Creativity

(A) "It took me reflecting on myself and how I wanted to show up and honour myself, that it was a gift for them to hear English spoken in a different accent. To know that they are training themselves to listen and communicate with everyone, that people from around

The Montessori Mission, by Charlotte Awdry

the world speak English in different accents. I give them the gift of being that teacher who has a different accent from their mom or whoever they interact with."
Tatenda Blessing Muchiriri (2021)

Tatenda spoke of how he came to realise that his accent and the unique lens of his lived experiences are gifts that he brings to the classroom.

- Encourage a conversation with your child which reflects upon the lives of others. They could draw from their own experience of diversity that they naturally experience living in a large city, or it could be the diversity within their classroom, family or friendship groups.
- In what ways do you celebrate diversity and inclusivity as a way of life within your family?

One lovely book for children to consider is, This Is How We Do It, by Matt Lamothe[1], which tells the story of seven different children around the world and their daily lives.

(B) Tatenda spoke about his beautiful NGO project Montessori on Wheels (IG: @ montessorionwheels), where he has converted an old school bus into a Montessori classroom to take to underserved communities who otherwise might not have access to Montessori education.

- When you think about the educational opportunities that are available in your area, do these serve all children? Are all children given equal access? And are their individual needs being met? Are resources equally distributed or is there an imbalance?
- Can you find any local initiatives that are working to redress this imbalance and to better meet the needs of under-served communities in your area?
- Do you have the knowledge, skills or time to volunteer for an initiative?
- How can you and your children get involved at a grassroots level to offer your gifts to serve others?

Montessori on Wheels is a global project that takes Montessori to underserved communities;, so get in touch with tatenda@montessorionwheels.com to take steps to bring the magic of Montessori on Wheels to where you are.

Share your thoughts... Email me sayhello@enrichingenvironments.com. Join me on Instagram & Facebook , follow me, tag my profile @enrichingenvironments and use the hashtag #montessorimission

Ochuko Prudence Daniels

Urhobo by birth and origin, and Yoruba by marriage, Prudence is the founder of Momahill Montessori in Lagos, Nigeria, an entrepreneur, a mother and a Parenting Educator. She is a powerful voice for Montessori in Africa and her work with children has received global recognition.

At Momahill Prudence has a Casa environment and Elementary, so all the way up to 12 years old. She is also the promoter of D'Parent's Prerogative platform, a group that helps parents navigate the parenting life using Montessori ideas.

She promotes women and youth entrepreneurship in her country through her RYE[2] Initiative, where she and her team voluntarily trained over 2000 youths in 2017 under the Lagos State Ministry of Women Affairs and Poverty Alleviation. And is also thinking of ways in which she can impact even younger children with her newest project, which will focus on coaching expectant mothers on how to raise a Montessori child from birth.

We begin the 10 Questions...

Charlotte:

Prudence has a great story of how Montessori came to her through her own children. Shall we start with that before we dive into the questions?

Prudence:

I stumbled into Montessori when I was looking for a good school for my children. We believe in good education in Africa, and even though it is not where it should be, things are getting better. I stumbled into a school where they were speaking about the total child, which caught my attention; I sold the idea of the school to my husband, and we agreed to send our first child there. It was very interesting to begin to learn about the Montessori activities, the practical life activities. The school always answered our questions, got us involved in what they were doing and why; it really caught my interest and, as time passed, I began to see the manifestation in my children.

Up until my children were six or seven, they never broke a glass at home, which I attribute to the careful ways they had been shown how to carry a pitcher, how to carry a tray, how to carry a glass of water, and then the pouring activities. For me, that was really interesting and I decided to query it more. So, a few years ago when that same school was opening up a training centre, I was interested because I love to learn and I wanted to practice. I worked with children voluntarily and I just wanted to have more knowledge about caring for children, looking after these beautiful gifts of God. And then I got hooked; the training was so transformational and very touching.

Many of my colleagues had regrets and how they would have raised their children otherwise. I had a few regrets, but I was also glad that I found Montessori when I did and this further enforced my drive to pursue it. I don't want to use the word wild but it is close to it.

I was wild about Montessori, to tell my friends and my church members; I wanted everyone to hear about Montessori and the impact of Montessori in the lives of little ones!

And our school is in its second year of the programme; we actually started during the pandemic. My training helped me to implement Montessori at home with my daughter, more than I did with my son because I didn't know as much then. So, that has actually transformed the way I relate with my children and how we practice Montessori at home.

Charlotte:

Montessori isn't accessible to every child, at every school in every country of the world; but the principles are so beautiful and so simple, we can do them at home without any Montessori training. We don't need or want parents to set up a Montessori environment in their home, but the pillars of respect and reverence for the child which are the absolute core of Montessori allows the soul of the child to unfold. We don't need to know anything about parenting, or children or Montessori to do those things.

There are so many cultures around the world who were already treating children with this reverence before it had a label. So, I think we can have it in every home, we just need to learn how to get rid of our own conditioning and beliefs. Because when we can find this wisdom and knowledge within ourselves, then we can offer it to our child as a gift.

Prudence:

Exactly. Even in my own culture, we do Montessori by default; so there are lots of parents doing activities that are culturally Montessori, it's just that the purpose is different. For example, families get their children to do chores from a very young age, they send them on errands. In Montessori, the "bring me game" in the Toddlers Community guides the child to participate and to be responsible for doing something. And in Montessori, we are doing that for cognitive and physical development. So, that is why I say that the purpose might be different, but we already do Montessori as a default.

1. What does Montessori mean to you?

Prudence:

That is a very beautiful question which is close to my heart. After I found Montessori it became a light, like a liberatory machine for the world, what we all need to be free. Montessori keeps me vibrant; if I was hungry, and you invited me to talk about Montessori, I don't think I would bother with food anymore. It is that bad, or let me say it is that good. Montessori to me is a national developmental programme and that is why I started my school. After my training I could have gone abroad to practice Montessori in a school where I would earn money, which when converted to my money made sense.

But I had a calling that Africa needed Montessori, Africa needed me to practice Montessori, to bring it to the children who might never encounter Montessori in their lifetime.

The Montessori Mission, by Charlotte Awdry

I am grateful to God that, in less than three years, we already have people who probably would never have come across Montessori. The majority of the families at my school today just say: "I was going by and I saw this beautiful place and I wanted to check it out." And then we get talking about Montessori and we start the on-boarding process. That is how it has been. So, more than 80% of our school families are people within the community who are curious to know what kind of school this is.

Charlotte:

So, they were not already-well versed in Montessori? That is really interesting and beautiful that you are bringing in people from your immediate community.

Prudence:

I remember I had to drive hours to bring my children to a Montessori school. So, I thought if there are people who won't even bother driving to a Montessori school, why don't we bring it to them?

They just walk in, and it's really tremendous, their testimonials are so humbling; I'm glad that I chose this path.

Charlotte:

Wow! I have got tears in my eyes. I love what you said right at the beginning, it's the light, it's freedom. That is what Montessori is.

2. What was your first light bulb moment on your Montessori journey?

Prudence:

During my training, it dawned on me that I am who I am now because my parents paid attention. I can just imagine that if my parents had had a glimpse of Montessori knowledge, it would have been more than a blast. So, for me, I feel that everybody should come across Montessori, everybody should encounter it. Especially in math; when we are studying about the line of mathematics from concrete to abstract, that line of preparation. Imagine, you have to begin from the sensorial, from language enrichment, and you are targeting mathematics, but you are here. How did Maria Montessori do it? This was over 110 years ago, how did she have all the answers then that are still valid, they still deliver results and it's a formula you can keep applying. For me, that is so mysterious and deep. And the enlightening grew when I started taking courses on each of the curriculum areas; that was it for me.

Charlotte:

You are so right; the indirect preparation for what is to come that happens in those early practical life materials, the early sensorial materials. Everything is building that beautiful, solid foundation so the child can do what they feel they need to do next. We can just observe and then we feel in our hearts what they need, we guide them through.

She was such a visionary. It is insane to think that was over 110 years ago, she saw the complete child, the wholeness, and she could see this vision of the whole human being, extraordinary.

3. In what ways does Montessori enrich the work that you do?

Prudence:
My work is Montessori, so there is nothing to be enriched; I am swimming in it, basking in it, everything is Montessori. There is no separate activity that Montessori has to enhance. But, personally, the whole transformation has influenced my personality, in terms of how I now respond to other adults, situations around me and especially children around me, and it has made me a better person.

Charlotte:
That really resonates deeply with me. I feel the same, that it has made me more of who I want to be; the way I want to give, the way I want to serve. It is extraordinary, it's a portal for all of us.

Prudence:
How you see the community; you burn for what you have to give to the community, to the people who really need those things. For example, I could have a better situation doing something else, but I enjoy working long hours aiding little ones to develop to normalcy and to become the best version of themselves. It is really transforming for me as a person, both in my work and in my life.

Charlotte:
I think you are right, in relationships, the way we interact with other adults, the way we handle conflict when it comes up in our life; whether it is someone being disrespectful to us, or somebody else, or it is our impatience when we are waiting in a really long queue at the supermarket; it makes us a better person.

I think it also draws out the richness in whatever our belief system or religious beliefs are; I think it just draws in so much richness from that as well. It becomes part of the fabric of our lives.

4. When was the first time a child taught you something about yourself that you weren't aware of?

Prudence:

I had a really rich parenting experience when my own children were little, and I wasn't even doing Montessori then. On one occasion, my son, who was about four, moved towards a light source and I saw him trying to poke a finger through. And I just ran, how a mother would respond to that kind of situation, I grabbed him and then realised that I had overreacted. I was already in tears and he saw my tears and started crying, which brought a deeper emotion to me than I was already experiencing. In retrospect, being in Montessori talks about the response, how the overall presence of the adult and the adult as a material in the classroom can actually influence the child. So, that came to light in that sense. Years later, I saw my son coaching his sister, who was about the same age, over the same incident. I saw that he was passing it down to his sister by saying, "This is very dangerous, you could get electrocuted." I wasn't even in Montessori then, so that for me was really enlightening to know that whatever you model to your children, they can become models of the same things you do, as long as they absorb what you have modelled before them. So, that is an experience that speaks to learning something about myself that a child actually taught me.

Charlotte:

It's a brilliant example. The older ones becoming Guides, whether it is in the home or the classroom, is just so beautiful to watch. And the bond that they have formed through doing that whether in their home or the classroom, is also beautiful to watch.

5. When was the last time a child taught you something about yourself that you weren't aware of?

Prudence:

This one is very funny. It happened recently when my boy came back home from school and I was insisting on something being done properly. And he said to me, "You know what? This is how I perceive this to be done but you perceive it in another way." Then he went further to say: "You might not see it in my own light because that is how perfectionists behave." And that just humbled me, hearing him pointing out to me that I'm being a bit too much in that scenario. That was really a reflective moment for me to pause and take a break and look inwards.

Charlotte:

Did you have your moment of reflection and then discuss it further? Or did you discuss it later? Or did nothing else need to be said?

Prudence:

I let that moment lie and we laughed about it. Then I went back to say, "Okay, at what point did you realise that I might be tending towards this, and why do you feel so?" So, we actually had a good discussion around that and it was healthy; and I was happy because if I wasn't in Montessori, I would have been offended, being the African that I am.

Charlotte:

It could seem disrespectful.

Prudence:

Yes, but because of the experience, training and the transformation, I saw it as something that I had to pause, reflect, and work on.

Charlotte:

I imagine that it is challenging; my children are only four and seven, but my seven year old is definitely challenging me with the: "That's not fair. You need to explain that." She questions me on my integrity. The example you have just given with your son, adolescents are actually at that place where they want to make the world a better place. So, we better be measuring up to whatever integrity we are calling them into. We have to measure up to that so it is great to hear that perspective of an adolescent— thank you for sharing that story.

6. When was the last time a child caught you out of integrity and questioned you on it?

Prudence:

I was driving at night with my daughter, who was around seven at the time. It was a little quiet because it was quite late and we were going home from a distant location where I had been working. And when we got to the last traffic light before a turn, I went through the red light, and my daughter asked, "Mum, why did you do that?" I said, "Don't worry, I am going to explain, let's get out of here first." When I moved further ahead, I took my time to explain to her that sometimes, at certain locations, especially at night, it is dangerous to wait at the traffic lights to pass because you could be attacked by robbers. That is not peculiar to everywhere but certain locations are just that dangerous sometimes. So, I had to explain that you just have to move on but you have to be very sure that the other sides are free for you to go so you don't get involved in an accident. And to that, she said, "But it wasn't green. You must move only when it is green." So, when we got home, I let her relax and we went over it again. I even involved my husband in the conversation and we were able to get her to understand that we don't just do that because we want to break the law. At certain times when it is not safe, you have to choose the safer option.

Charlotte:

So, in that absolute stage of morality. Development and moral justice in that age is so important. How much did she know about the potential dangers at that age? How did you explain to her that it could be dangerous in certain parts without scaring her? How did you have that conversation?

Prudence:

There is a story about how my husband and I got attacked once. I was pregnant with her when we were driving home one night, and robbers stopped us at gunpoint. It was very traumatic and is not something I want to go back to. We managed to get ourselves out of the car unhurt before it was taken. She has been told this story because my little boy remembers it clearly, he was about three; and he tells her about it. So, I had to relate it to that, "Remember the story about how we were robbed when I was pregnant with you? We don't want that kind of thing to happen. We stopped and that is how they gained access to the car, took our valuables and the car." So she had that story, and was then able to relate.

Every family at one point or another has experienced that kind of thing or has heard about it. In school, they also teach about how you can be safe, like don't open the door to strangers, don't speak to strangers, and things like that. So, it wasn't so much of a difficult scenario to explain myself out of. She was able to understand that at certain times, you just have to pick the safer option. African children are pretty smart, because they experience a lot of things at a very young age. Life happens and they get to see a whole lot. We are still growing and developing in terms of child protection, so sadly there are a lot of children who are exposed to things that they are not supposed to be.

Charlotte:

That is the hard part, isn't it? When you are doing the work that you are doing, it can feel overwhelming, because you are one person with one school and once your heart goes into this work, you want to help everyone. Thank you for sharing that difficult story.

7. How did you explain yourself when you were out of integrity?

Prudence:

Even in recent times, when we move in certain places that are not well lit, she says,

"Mummy do you think it's okay to wait?" She remembers and asks, "Do you think it's okay to wait? Or do you want to check if it's all clear, so we can just drive through?" She remembers that story very well, but now with a better understanding to be able to advise on where we should go or not.

8. What is your favourite Dr. Montessori quote?

Prudence:

When you wake me up from my sleep, the first Dr. Montessori quote I am going to think about is, "Free the child's potential, and you will transform him into the world." [1] And that is something that drives me to do what I do in my school because we are helping the child to liberate their inner being, so they can get to wherever they want to go and accelerate whatever they want to do.

Charlotte:

Nothing will hold them back.

Prudence:

Serving the needs of those children, doing what you ought to do as a Montessori adult.

9. What is your deepest desire for Montessori in the future?

Prudence:

That is a huge question for me! A few months ago when I was driving to school, I had a nudge in my spirit that said something to me about bringing Montessori to Africa in a way that it becomes a legacy: Let me use the words that actually occurred to me on that day:

"Prudence, you need to build a Montessori village," a mini city that is everything Montessori. Children can come from far and near, whether they can afford to pay or not, to be developed and freed. You know how you let a kite fly? Just let go. Have a gigantic Montessori facility with every child developmental space available to aid African children to be able to develop in a proper way.

When I heard that in my spirit I was like, "How on earth am I going to do that?" Just like when I started the school, I didn't have enough capacity in terms of financing or other trained adults to support me in my dream. But I just knew that for me to change my world, I should just begin from where I was. And I say, "My world", because the world is so huge, so starting from your little space makes it the whole world. That is how I dove in without having all the finances, without having all the trained adult

The Montessori Mission, by Charlotte Awdry

support, and without having even the materials to work with. I just dove in and began to build on it. So, I am thinking about it in the same way; I know that it is achievable because I established the school from absolutely nothing, and thank God, the Black Montessori Education Fund (BMEF)[2], was very supportive because it was not very easy to do. And so, to think about the Montessori village for Africa in Nigeria is a really big dream. When you go around, you see a lot of schools with Montessori attached to the names. I remember in my training, I was told that Montessori did not patent the name because it was at a time of war, it was chaotic, and there was gender bias. So, everyone can use it and that is the way it is here, everyone can use the name Montessori, but they are not actually developing the child's potential as they should be. So, my dream is to have a humongous facility for children to come from far and near; have a training centre to train adults to be able to guide the children, and to just keep going at making a better Africa in the next 25, 50, 100 years or more.

Charlotte:

Wow! That is so special and achievable. As you said before your school, everything seemed impossible. Nelson Mandela said, "Everything seems impossible until it is done."

Prudence:

That is my little secret on my pillow when I sleep at night.

Charlotte:

It is in your prayers, I can feel that from your heart and from your song. I know that that feeling means that it is going to happen, you can feel from your energy that it is going to happen. And so, Prudence, you spoke of a Montessori village, with children coming from near and far, whether or not they can afford it, that is what we can aspire to, isn't it? I was listening to a podcast the other day talking about how in the Netherlands Montessori is part of the public system, so children can attend a government, non-fee paying Montessori school. Wouldn't that be incredible if that was the norm? As you said, if governments offer authentic Montessori education as a way of life, as part of their commitment to the people of their country. Whether it's Nigeria, the UK, Dubai, that is a legacy.

Prudence:

I want to point something out. As a school, we must work with the state curriculum. I was shocked to see that every aspect of the government curriculum had Montessori elements built into it, and I was shocked to my bones. But it is not implemented in the public schools and I am wondering: how do you draw up a curriculum that is not implemented as a state or a nation? It means that the government within my country has the right people in place, they have consulted with probably the right personnel who have given the right advice, and then documented these things. The gap between that and the child is implementation and it is that gap I really hunger to fill as a practitioner.

Charlotte:

What do you think are the barriers to that? If the intention is there, and it is written as the curriculum for Nigerian public schools, why is it not being delivered? Why is it not being implemented?

Prudence:

I think that maybe some consultants have done their work and moved on, and then the next level of people who are in charge have no clue. Maybe professionals need to be on that board, I really don't know. But I was really surprised to see that there were so many Montessori elements in the curriculum and I know that is not what is being practiced in public schools.

I would really like to see Montessori as a public charter in my country and beyond and in other African countries, so that the children are better served, because if you really want a great country, you need to invest in the children.

Charlotte:

Nigeria is booming, and building a great country comes from the people that are there. It's logical that we begin with the earliest years to build a great country or nation.

10. What do you see is your role in achieving this desire?

Prudence:

So, I need to have 10 other Prudences to be able to run this and then I will be able to serve the government on what they need! Like I said earlier, start with your little space; I believe in starting your little corner. There is a song I used to know about a missionary when I was much younger. It says something about you in your small corner and I in mine, together we are working and making this world a better place. So, I think my role is to just keep doing what I am doing, serving Montessori children in my space, expanding it as much as possible, enlightening more adults and introducing them to the Montessori world. Opening up training opportunities for them because the more trained adults we have, the more children we will be able to serve. My role will be to do as much as I can, and keep spreading it until every home, every family is touched with the right developmental methods.

The Montessori Mission, by Charlotte Awdry

Charlotte:

I can feel that stardust from you, as you said from family to family, I think there is some Prudence stardust there that you can sprinkle.

Prudence:

We are already doing that in some way, like in our school currently. I take delight in on-boarding fresh parents, those who have never heard about Montessori and they have no bias about, "Oh, I want my child to write at age three or four. I want my child to do mathematics or science."

I take delight in helping them to understand what this pedagogy really means and how it is supposed to impact us as a family, and then how we respect the child, because respect is one huge part of our culture that is missing in Africa. We have a huge respect culture that disrespects the child.

So, there has to be that trajectory, there has to be a change of that aspect to be able to see the child for who the child really is; as Montessori states, a child who deserves to be loved and respected. A child who deserves an explanation for their own communication if they actually need those explanations. We have to be able to bring them into our conversations, bring them into our decision-making and bring them into our most respected zones where we usually prohibit children from.

Charlotte:

Isn't that interesting? A culture of respect that disrespects children.

Prudence:

I hear parents telling me, "I'm not going to bring my child if you are not going to discipline them." Of course, not understanding what discipline is from a Montessori perspective.

Charlotte:

We are starting to define the word discipline from such different points.

Prudence:

We are not going to sit the child down to work long hours to be able to achieve a particular task, or whoop the child on their bum or their palms. We are just going to make your child develop naturally and we are going to help them to be the best version of themselves. We are going to make them be responsible, they will be able to hold their heads up high, and nobody is going to be able to put them down.

Charlotte:

You said that most of your parents are ones who have no bias either way, with Montessori. Do you find that the traditional approach to education is more dominant? Or do you feel it is progressing a little?

Prudence:

Oh, yes. It is getting better because there is more enlightenment. More younger parents in their 30s are actually more respectful to their children. I think because of the global space, a lot of them are online, they are reading about parenting. Of course, my mother wouldn't have gone online to learn parenting skills, it is what her grandmother passed down to her. So, things are changing, but not as fast as they should. We are having that conversation and gladly, we have parents who are actually willing to learn. They come in with that mindset and I say to them, "If you have problems, you can always come back and we can help you understand how to deal with it in a Montessori way." And it has been working; I have had at least a couple of parents come up to me to say, "Oh, I have trouble getting my child dressed, because they won't wear this or that." And I go, "Okay, so here is a choice issue, make a limited choice option, and then let them choose." And they come back to say, "Oh, it's working." So, we actually have parents who are open-minded, and they are ready to learn, and they are getting results and are happy with the results that they are getting as well.

Charlotte:

That is the best feedback, isn't it? When we can give parents the gift of trusting themselves and going, "Okay, I know all of this inside myself, but we are just here to help them see what they know already in their heart without the side of it where we are just doing the same as other people have done before." Your vision is so inspiring and you know from your own experience what can be achieved. Anything is possible.

Prudence:

I believe it!

ỌMIỌVWỌ

(Urhobo Nursing Mother)

BY CHOVWE INISIAGBO-OGBE:

Ọmiọvwọ,

The nursing mother

With her new born

Cuddled in her hands

Bathed with encomiums

Joy is her name

Pride for her crown

Lavished with gifts

For this task of nature

Wherein her womb

She nurtured nine months

An embryo till birth

Freshly dressed after labour

Made up face maybe

Fed with choice food

To regain all losses

Nourishment and baby

Family , friends

Neighbours , well-wishers

Visit in droves

A queenly treatment

Being a mother

Does not come easy!

A peek into the world of Prudence

Images: Left to right
(1) This piece is dear to my heart. It was done by my niece Chinonso Akpati. It depicts the love and support of a mother. And my school community holds this dear. **(2)** My previous career as interior designer 2018. **(3)** Udje Cultural Dance Of Urhobo Land Painting by Nefe Ogodo – I love this dance from when I was young and its still a delight to watch.

The Montessori Mission, by Charlotte Awdry

Images: From top, left to right

(1) *Opening of MomaHill Montessori School 2020.*
(2) *Preparations for the opening of Momahill Montessori School 2020.*
(3) *During Montessori training in 2018.*

Reflective practice

1. Journal

"In my own culture, we do Montessori by default; so there are lots of parents doing activities that are culturally Montessori, it's just that the purpose is different. For example, families get their children to do chores from a very young age, they send them on errands. In Montessori, the "bring me game" in the Toddlers Community guides the child to participate and to be responsible for doing something. And in Montessori, we are doing that for cognitive and physical development. So, that is why I say that the purpose might be different, but we already do Montessori as a default."
Ochuko Prudence Daniels (2021)

With this in mind, acknowledge the ways in which you are already practising Montessori principles of developing autonomy, a sense of community and responsibility in your child.

2. Embodiment

"This one is very funny. It happened recently when my boy came back home from school and I was insisting on something being done properly. And he said to me, "You know what? This is how I perceive this to be done but you perceive it in another way... You might not see it in my own light because that is how perfectionists behave."
Ochuko Prudence Daniels (2021)

Prudence offered us this touching and funny story of how her son called to her attention that she was being a perfectionist.

Can you recall a time when your child has playfully brought your attention to one of your personality traits? How did that feeling of joyful connection with your child feel in your body? The feeling that your child is aware of your idiosyncrasies and accepts you as you are?

3. Creativity

Prudence's passion and commitment to her purpose is infectious!

Reflect upon your passion and purpose in your life.

- Do you have one broad vision?
- How do you keep yourself on track with this vision?
- Do you have a vision board or mind map, a visual plan that you refer to?
- Do you have a mastermind group with friends or peers where you share ideas and uplift each other in your respective visions?
- How often do you look at and revise your vision where needed?
- In what ways can you imbue your passion and purpose into all that you do?
- For a child aged 6 and above, how can you support your child to follow their passion and develop their sense of purpose?

Share your thoughts... Email me sayhello@enrichingenvironments.com. Join me on Instagram & Facebook , follow me, tag my profile @enrichingenvironments and use the hashtag #montessorimission

CHAPTER 10

Sid Mohandas

Born and raised in India, Sid Mohandas is a former Montessori Educator and trainer, a guest lecturer at Middlesex University in the UK and the founder of two platforms, The Male Montessorian (www.themalemontessorian.com) and Montistory (@montistory101).

He is currently doing his doctorate at Middlesex University which is an investigation into the gendered workforce in the Montessori space.

Sid is a familiar face in the Montessori world and has a unique perspective on Montessori, which I am excited for him to share.

We begin the 10 Questions...

Charlotte:

Before we dive into the questions Sid, could you tell us a bit more about your doctorate at Middlesex University, and how it all began?

Sid:

Absolutely. I was doing a Masters in Sweden on cell and molecular biology when I came across a friend who was a psychotherapist; and she shared with me how many of the things that adults go through during their adulthood have their roots in childhood. This got me thinking about my own childhood and the struggles that I had as an adult; and I then started searching for different pedagogical approaches, which led me to Montessori. That is how my journey in early childhood started. It has been a number of years now and currently, as you said, I am doing a doctorate, exploring and investigating how a gendered workforce emerges in the Montessori context by using post human and new material theories. So, it has been quite a journey.

Charlotte:

Amazing! Tell us more about your doctorate. So, when you say Montessori in the gendered workplace, what is the research you are doing?

Sid:

Traditionally, Montessori is framed as gender neutral and there is the idea that the classroom is gender neutral. My doctorate is trying to unpack and unravel, by using different theories, how every encounter we have is riddled with gender relationality and the subtle ways that gender emerges within everyday encounters.

Charlotte:

It sounds really fascinating. What have you found so far?

Sid:

I think the dominant narrative is that we need more men. My research troubles with that in the sense that when we focus on this idea that we need more men to rescue early childhood, it masks and obscures a lot of other problematic aspects that are happening within the classroom, in terms of sustaining patriarchy in other ways. Simply having men in the classroom does not really address some of the gender inequalities that we experience, and quite often men who come into the sector experience what you call, "the glass escalator", they climb up into leadership and management roles quickly, which is problematic.

Charlotte:

So, simply bringing in more male Guides isn't the answer then?

Sid:

No. It's not. We don't need simplistic narratives around gender, it just doesn't help. We need to expose everyone to gender-sensitive pedagogy and understand how complex gender emerges in the classroom.

Charlotte:

Thank you so much for the insight, your doctorate sounds fascinating. When will you be finished?

Sid:

My doctorate should be finished in April next year. I have already published a number of papers and chapters; and some of my work is already available in journals and in books.

Charlotte:

Thank you for sharing that with us. Now, I think we are ready to dive into the 10 questions; I am so interested to hear your perspective!

1. What does Montessori mean to you?

Sid:

For me, Montessori is about responsiveness. Now, this may seem controversial, but to me, Montessori is not exclusively about the child. And by that I mean it is not about viewing the child as an isolated entity, but instead seeing childhood as inextricably entangled in relations, and shifting relations. It is about attuning to those situated contextual relations and engaging in practises of care. Even if we look into the history of the Montessori method, we realise that it emerged as a response to very specific political, economic and social issues and was enormously shaped by Montessori's own political consciousness and her feminist activism. So, I believe Montessori is a response to pedagogy and it should be about responding to contemporary childhood issues, responding to situated injustices, enacting care and enabling creative capacities. That is what Montessori means to me.

Charlotte:

That is beautiful. You touched on her feminist activism which is something that I think a lot of us are revisiting. I studied 10 years ago, and I didn't really grasp her strong feminist activism at the time.

2. What was your first light bulb moment on your Montessori path?

Sid:

Well, I don't know if it was the first one, but it is a very important light bulb moment for me. As a newly qualified teacher, I remember going through the base of meticulously following the album for my presentations. So much so, that I sometimes became oblivious to the children in front of me and their worlds. But as I became more attuned, I realised that I could adapt the presentations based on where each child was at, without losing sight of this rationale. However, my view on presentations considerably changed when I was put in charge of a classroom of 38 children! I realised that my role as the arbiter of the materials and learning was displaced, with the role often taken up by children in the classroom.

The children were absolutely capable, and always already in modes of learning, whether I was overseeing the learning or not, learning was constantly happening. So, decentering the adult in the classroom, and seeing the child's capacities and abilities to unfold was definitely a critical light bulb moment for me.

Charlotte:

As you said, decentering the adult and that magical time in the year when the older children are doing most of the presentations is just incredible. It feels like that is at the core of Montessori when the children actually take over and run the classroom themselves. That is really what we are hoping to gift them; we have decentered ourselves enough that they have the freedom, the confidence and the joy to lead others. My daughter is in Montessori Elementary and is the youngest in the class, she's just seven. And I see more and more that she is being guided so much by the other children who are 8 and 9; and it is really incredible.

Sid:

It is really magical to witness that transformation; the mixed age classroom is just phenomenal.

3. In what ways does Montessori enrich the work that you do?

Sid:

Montessori has definitely enlarged my capacity to care and be cared for. One of the things that really struck me when I first came to Montessori was the deep respect, trust and reverence she had for the child. I grew up in a time when it was believed that children should be seen and not heard.

Very often, when it comes to education, you can hear the voices of the parents, teachers, policymakers, and politicians, while the child is often the silent recipient of all things; everything is done for and to them.

Therefore the idea of granting the child freedom, voice and agency touched the little child within me that wished to be heard and listened to. This is great and this is what education should be. However, what is truly transformative is when that respect, trust and care permeates all layers and tissues of the Montessori experience, especially the teacher training programme, and the teacher-training experience.

My teacher training in the Foundation Degree programme at the former MCI was quite a remarkable and transformative experience. To experience that deep-seated, respect, trust and care from the tutors gave me something tangible to hold on to, especially as I did not experience Montessori as a child.

How do we give that Montessori experience that isn't embedded in the adult Montessori teacher training experience or teacher preparation experience? Sadly, I have come to realise that what I experienced is not the norm. The dominant approach to training and preparation of the adult in Montessori continues to be disconnected from the philosophy that drives our practice with children. So, students are treated as blank slates. The assessment approaches and frameworks are gradually top down, and student agency is quite limited.

I really think that for the Montessori experience, there needs to be a seamless practice of the philosophy across the boundaries, it is not just a childhood experience, but it needs to permeate all different aspects of the Montessori community. Montessori has really opened up possibilities to care and be cared for.

Charlotte:
I love how you said, we can't offer this respect and care and reverence to children and not actually offer it to the adults we are interacting with as well. The parents that we are interacting with and families that we are working with, all have their own inner child that needs to be tended to.

Sid:
Absolutely; and the staff as well. I previously worked at a phenomenal Montessori school that had great practice with the children; it was a packaway Montessori setting, and we had to come in early to set up the classroom. And during this process, the leadership and manager would be running around shouting at the staff but as soon as the children came in, everyone had to be calm.

This dualism was so wrong; how can you talk about caring and loving and being respectful to children when you are not being that way with adults? We really need to address that within the Montessori community because there is a problem.

Charlotte:

That lack of congruency in following our practice all the way through; it being a way of life. I don't know if you are familiar with the Imago dialogue? It is a really incredible way of communicating to ensure that everyone is heard in a conversation and their needs are being met. When I was in Cape Town, South Africa, I used the Imago dialogue in the classroom. The racial structure there is so complex, and in the classroom, there would typically be a White lead, and then the classroom assistant and all the other staff would be non-White. It wasn't possible to have an equal conversation, so we used the Imago dialogue. So, I completely agree that every single person we come in contact with, and particularly the people who are working the longest hours and the people who are being paid the least, are the people who most need to be heard.

Sid:

Absolutely. So true.

4. When was the first time a child taught you something about yourself that you weren't aware of?

Sid:

Not so much about myself, but about life. And definitely not the first time, but I was reminded of this encounter recently, when we were preparing for the Technology Summit with Montessori Europe. At one of the preschools that I worked at, cameras were incorporated as part of the daily life of the classroom. They were used as a valid mode of minute making, which involved children taking photos and then explaining them which led to a dialogue. One time I was going through the photos in the school camera, and I came across these blurred images of a raised platform in the garden area. I knew who had taken these photos, so I took it back to the child and they shared that the raised platform was a spot that they would go and sit when they felt really sad and missed their mom. It was also the platform that they sat on when they were waiting expectantly for their parents to come back.

That really touched me and it underscored the fact that children are constantly making sense of their world and actively making connections and meanings, whether we know it or not.

It gave me a new appreciation for independence and being okay with not knowing. And it really helped me to move away from thinking that the child can be fully known or fully figured out. It taught me that it is okay and valuable to not know, and I think Montessori herself talks about this in creative development in the child, where she talks about how whilst it is beautiful to witness the child learning, what is happening within the child isn't for us to know. And then she says the secret of childhood belongs to the child, which I think is fabulous. That place of not knowing is a good place to be, and is something I learned from my encounter there.

Charlotte:
How old was the child who had taken the photo?

Sid:
Possibly three.

Charlotte:
Wow! There is a great quote about children needing to have secrets and needing to have an inner world to themselves that we are not prying into. I guess in modern Western society, it is the opposite; we are trying to schedule them and make sure that every single bit of time in their education is accounted for. My early years were very wild in terms of just going into the garden for hours and playing in the fields, probably doing all types of dangerous things that my parents didn't really know what we were getting up to. And in just one generation, we have lost that.

Sid:
That space to be has been lost.

Charlotte:
I am lucky enough here that although we live in a small apartment there is a park right opposite us, ten metres away. I let the children go out, and they are confident enough to go out and just play in the park on their own, so I can clean the house and cook. It is so great and they come back famished and thirsty, really grubby with scraped knees from climbing trees. I am giving them as much as I can, the opportunity to take risks and to make mistakes. I don't really know what they are getting up to, but I just trust that they are being kind to everyone that they encounter. And I think they are. I love that story, it is so important for our children to have that little bit of privacy for themselves; we don't need to micromanage their time or know everything about them. It takes a deep level of trust in them, but trust in ourselves that we are doing the right thing as parents.

The Montessori Mission, by Charlotte Awdry

5. When was the last time a child taught you something about yourself that you weren't aware of?

Sid:

This again, wasn't the last time, but it does stand out. To give you some context, I was working at a nursery that was deemed outstanding by OFSTED and they were quite over the top about safeguarding policies and managing risk. They would force children to walk on hard surfaces and permit them to only run on grass; and they made children run outdoors in the same direction, so they wouldn't bump into each other. Interestingly, the nursery had more accidents than any other place that I had ever worked at, because we were managing risks for them, rather than allowing them to take risks and assess risks for themselves. We even had elaborate instructions for the phrases we could use with children when risk was involved. For instance, if you found a child doing something that involved physical risks, you were expected to approach a child and say something like, "I am really worried that you will bump into your friend and hurt yourself." That sort of language was so ingrained into us as Educators. Fast forward, and I carried these habits and practises to the next setting that I went to. At this nursery, there was a four-year-old girl who just loved pushing boundaries; she loved doing things that made most adults feel uneasy. It was just how she was and she was also a very skilled tree climber; she would go to heights that you wouldn't expect a four-year-old child to go to. And there was one time that she kept going up the tree in the garden, and I was standing below and regurgitating these formulaic phrases that I had without even realising that I was doing it, and she just turned around and looked at me and said, "You are always worried, aren't you?" This made me pause and then it made me rethink the language that I was using with the children. It enabled me to see that risk-averse language had become part of my daily vocabulary practice. It also got me thinking of better ways of using language that helped children to manage risk by themselves and for themselves.

Charlotte:

That is brilliant. There is nothing like a four year old to tell you what's what, they are brilliant. Did she manage to get down safely with your strict instructions?

Sid:

I realised that I didn't need to instruct her; she was more skilled than most people I know.

Charlotte:

When children aren't used to being spoken to in that language of, "Slowly, gently, carefully," it can be really strange to them. My daughter Olivia said that to me a couple of weeks ago, when we were with friends in the park. One of the adults kept on saying, "Careful, careful, careful," and Olivia asked me, "Why is she saying careful the whole time? Why doesn't she just let her concentrate?" I have really tried not to say 'careful' to Olivia and Harry so they learn their own limits, but it is funny how they notice and pick up on everything.

Sid:

Especially when you keep on saying careful, you are actually distracting the child.

Charlotte:

Children show us what we need to know.

6. When was the last time a child caught you out of integrity, and questioned you on it?

Sid:

Well, it was my niece, who is in Australia; she was 12 at the time. I video chat with her once in a while, where we have extensive conversations about all kinds of topics. This one time, we were chatting and I decided to take a screenshot of our images while having the conversation. I don't have many photos of her with me, so I just decided to take a screenshot. And after we chatted and hung up, I shared this screenshot with her. She responded saying, "I like that photo of me, but you didn't have my consent to take a screenshot." I am big on consent, and that moment was a real learning moment for me; things that we take for granted.

7. How did you explain yourself when you were out of integrity?

Sid:

Well, I did not see that coming at all. I was really proud of her for calling me out on it, to be able to stand up for herself and what she believed. Of course, the response to her was that I apologised and ensured that I would respect her wish in the future. But there wasn't any explanation needed; she had totally owned it.

Charlotte:

How powerful for a 12 year old to know her boundaries so clearly; what was okay and what was not okay. It's great!

Sid:

It definitely needs to be part of the educational experience, they should know consent from a very young age.

The Montessori Mission, by Charlotte Awdry

8. What is your favourite Dr. Montessori quote?

Sid:

I have one written here: "I give very few lessons on how to give lessons, lest my suggestions - becoming stereotypes and parodied- should turn into obstacles instead of help. The directress is dealing with different personalities; and it therefore becomes more a question of how she should orient herself in what is for her new world, rather than any rigid and absolute rules."[1] It is so refreshing to read this, especially in the context where there is the tendency to get caught up in the mechanistic implementation of the approach without really grasping the spirit of Montessori practice and philosophy.

Recently, I have been reading The Montessori Method with a couple of my friends. If you read the first few chapters of The Montessori Method, you find that Montessori was, in fact, fighting against this very mechanistic, reductionist approach to 'scientific education' at the time. Where they had all the techniques, tools and instruments to measure learning and development, but lacked a deep sense of knowing that only came through what Montessori refers to as the intimate relationship between the Educator and the child.

Charlotte:

Thank you for bringing that to our attention because we get so caught up. Different training colleges argue about how we should be presenting a particular piece of work when we are just losing, as you so beautifully said, the spirit of Montessori or even the spirit of the child in front of us, if we are just presenting in the same way. We want to be a gift to the child, not just in the way we present the pink tower. A colleague of mine got a new classroom at the start of this academic year, and she said, "I hope I am doing these children justice, and doing this classroom justice, I just feel like I am drowning." And I said to her, "Just your presence in that environment is a gift. The children don't hope for anything more than just seeing you. Even if you don't present anything, don't worry, just being with them and accepting them is more powerful."

But we all remember what it is like, that first term of the academic year with a new classroom. It is really hectic. So many Montessorians that I have spoken to talk about us moving away from this formulaic approach to the materials, for us all to focus on the spirit of Montessori, on the spirit of the child, and what really is the essence of what she was seeking to create through her work.

9. What is your deepest desire for Montessori in the future?

Sid:

My deepest desire is for Montessori to be in a continuous place of reconfiguring, for the Montessori community to be brave enough to read Montessori through contemporary critical theories and challenge some of its very core tenets. I am personally drawn to the works of feminist and biologist, Donna Haraway. She has this phrase called "staying with the trouble", which means coming to a place of being able to hold controversies and contradictions together without having to smooth them out. I think that kind of smoothing not only erases the problematic aspects of Montessori, but it also takes away opportunities to what decolonial scholar, Maria Lugones, called deep coalition. I think it is perfectly okay that Montessori is imperfect. The approach is imperfect. And I think perfection of a pedagogy should not be something that we try to keep as our goal. As soon as it becomes a perfect approach, or we think it is perfect, it will stop being pliable, responsive, and lively. I think that constant reconfiguring is something that I hope will be the future of Montessori.

Charlotte:

Do you think we are all brave enough to do it? Pre-COVID, the world was so different from what we now need and what children need. Around the world there are more children living in poverty than ever before, more women below the poverty line and even more inequality than there was before COVID; the global majority are in a worse position. So, what can we do in Montessori to really give ourselves a shake if that is what we need to reconfigure? What do you see that we need to do on a micro level and a macro level as Montessori collaborators?

Sid:

I don't see it happening at an institutional level; I have lost a bit of hope and trust with the institutions to make shifts. I feel a lot of hope from a grassroots level and how Montessorians are coming together. The Montessori Everywhere project is a great example of how we can come together and collaborate. What I said earlier about Maria Lugones' term of 'deep coalition', if we want to counter and respond to injustice, coming together and holding each other is very important.

Charlotte:

Coming together and holding each other; that is really lovely.

The Montessori Mission, by Charlotte Awdry

10. What do you see is your role in achieving this desire?

Charlotte:

So where do you fit in the reconfiguration of Montessori?

Sid:

In many ways, I see my role as what the scholar Sara Ahmed refers to as a feminist killjoy; as someone who speaks uncomfortable and necessary truths, but also as someone who thinks with, stands with, becomes with others, not as a unitary singular person but it is always a collective doing. I think critically engaging with Montessori is important. It's not a bad thing that I critique the Montessori approach because I love Montessori; I critique it because I believe Montessori deserves a future. I think critique ensures that Montessori will continue to be a dynamic, vibrant, responsible approach, and not a stagnant method. But of course, critique by itself is not enough if it doesn't also entail creation. The feminist scholar, Professor Rosi Braidotti talks about the marriage between critique and creation, bringing together critiquing creation and how that productive partnership is very important in our activism. I think we also need to consider alternative ways of thinking and doing. The truth is though, that Western scientific theories and theories of dead White European scholars prevail.

Charlotte:

I have heard this expression so much recently, and I just love it so much: we are just listening to dead White men.

Sid:

It's sad really. It is so coded into the way we think, and live and die in the world. Other ways of living and dying, as in the words of Donna Haraway, have become unthinkable, unavailable to us to think. Part of what I am doing and interested in is bringing these critical ways of thinking into the realm of Montessori practice. Because we can get so stuck in, Montessori is the best way and Montessori is the best practice, that we just can't see outside that narrow lens. I think it is very important for us to be relevant, but also be attuned to what Montessori was initially all about. Her approach was all about justice, care, and responding to injustice.

So, we have to respond to injustice in the 21st century. It is going to look different because the injustices are more complex, but lots of things that were not made known during her time are now available to us as a result of digital networking and digital technologies.

Like I said earlier, I have recently published a few papers where you apply some of these theories to open out investigations in Montessori classrooms and to enable thinking in practising Montessori differently, but most importantly to enable a difference within Montessori practice.

Charlotte:

I am interested, how is your work generally received in the Montessori community? I know Barbara Isaacs and you are really good friends, and she said to me, "I love how Sid always challenges me to look at things in a different way." But not everyone in the world is as open as Barbara.

Sid:

It is sad that it took the death of George Floyd being aired through a mobile device to shock people into thinking about it, when it is not anything new for the Black community. I think people are becoming more receptive, but at the same time, there is a huge resistance within the Montessori community, especially people who are trying to conserve and protect a particular version of Montessori. They don't want to hear that there are issues related to Whiteness. But we need to address it, we can't be preoccupied with "Oh, Montessori is all perfect and good," we have to talk about the problems. As I said, Montessori deserves a future.

Charlotte:

Montessori has bad press. Even if we just look at Instagram, using the hashtag Montessori brings up pages and pages of these perfect shelves in a cream and beige sitting room, with a White child going to the shelf, taking work and putting everything back where it belongs. And it really bothers me because everything in my home is accessible to the children, but I won't pan the camera around so you can see the chaos I am living in. It is a home for young children so I want them to feel cosy and at home, I don't want it to feel regimented, it shouldn't be like that.

Sid:

That was Montessori's original idea, the child's house should be where they feel at home. When you look back into historical images of Montessori classrooms, if we were to judge those classrooms by the manicured standards we have today, they would fail miserably.

That sense of beauty that we have constructed doesn't help either the practitioner or the child. We are just imposing a certain aesthetic for the sake of us, not for the sake of the children.

Charlotte:

It is a White middle-class aesthetic as well; it is not culturally relevant.

Sid:

Absolutely. There is an aesthetic that is very much shaped by middle-class sensibilities. If we go to traditional, earlier settings where things aren't as muted, that shows us the contrast in terms of class sensibilities.

Charlotte:

I am going to go a bit off topic here Sid, but I would love to know how you came to be involved in feminism? Was it before you came to Montessori?

Sid:

Initially when I first came into Montessori, I was really troubled by the under representation of men; and the narratives that surrounded the recruitment of men were very problematic. Women and communities of colour were framed in very negative terms, as a deficit, and there was this narrative that men could come in and bring balance.

It is often referred to as recuperative masculinity politics: if you have men, you can recuperate early years and help boys and girls who are underachieving. It is a narrative which automatically frames women as a deficit.

At the same time, it also promotes a very heteronormative model, that only if you have a man and a woman together is a family or society complete. There are lots of longitudinal studies that have been done that show queer families are equally as effective, loving and amazing as any other family. So, those issues actually got me thinking about gender and how it was being framed. The first time I read about feminist research was through the work of Glenda MacNaughton, who wrote a book called Rethinking gender and early childhood education (2001). In that she uses feminist post-structuralist theory, which considers how language shapes the gendered realities of children. So, that was my segue into feminist research and feminist thinking, although feminism has always been part of my life.

Charlotte:

How did that come to be? Was it from your parents or upbringing?

Sid:

Well, my mother was a Professor and Dean of the Political Science department in a University in India. And growing up I heard stories of her experiences of being a woman in a male-dominated context; the misogyny and sexism she experienced. It used to make me really angry, and so that feminist rage was very much part of my childhood.

Charlotte:

That is so interesting. Thank you for telling us how it all began. It is interesting you said about the longitudinal studies about queer families raising children. I was listening to a podcast where they were discussing how all different types of families can raise children. There is this myth that single mothers can't raise boys, which places the woman in deficit. I have a daughter and a son and this narrative is always in the back of my mind like, "Oh, is Harry going to be in deficit in some way because I am a single Mum?" That belief is so entrenched. What they were saying on this podcast is that it is simply not true, there are so many single parents; so this belief that they are somehow in deficit from being raised by a single mother is just not the case.

Sid:

It also places a particular model of masculinity on men. Not all men subscribe to traditional masculine ways of being. Even when I was in the nursery, there was an expectation that I was the disciplinarian. They would say "I'll take you to Mr. Sid." I started the Male Montessorian in 2015 as a response to these problematic narratives around men in early childhood, to have a more complex view of childhood, and gender.

Charlotte:

It is so interesting and thought-provoking, thank you Sid.

A peek into the world of Sid

Images:
(Left) *During training at Montessori Centre International, London.* **(Right)** *Art by Savi Aawarkar, Dalit couple wearing sputum pots around their neck, Mixed media*

Sid's chosen poem:

The Cost of Living

BY ARUNDHATI ROY

To love. To be loved.

To never forget your own insignificance.

To never get used to the unspeakable violence

And the vulgar disparity of life around you.

To seek joy in the saddest places.

To pursue beauty to its lair.

To never simplify what is complicated

Or complicate what is simple.

To respect strength, never power.

Above all, to watch.

To try and understand.

To never look away.

And never, never to forget.

Reflective practice

1. Journal

"Montessori has definitely enlarged my capacity to care and be cared for. One of the things that really struck me when I first came to Montessori was the deep respect, trust and reverence she had for the child." **Sid Mohandas (2021)**

With this beautiful quote in mind, consider…

- What in your life has enlarged your capacity to care, and to be cared for?
- What evokes deep respect, trust and reverence in you and from you?

2. Embodiment

"At the same time, it also promotes a very heteronormative model, that only if you have a man and a woman together, is a family or society complete. There are lots of longitudinal studies that have been done that show queer families are equally as effective, loving and amazing as any other family." **Sid Mohandas (2021)**

Sid brilliantly challenges our way of looking at the world, and the narratives that we have grown up with which can often be the ones that we do not question.

- Take a moment to feel into the last time you felt that a long-held belief of yours had been questioned. This could be either directly in conversation, or something you watched or read.

What bodily sensations did you experience? It is not unusual to experience a closure when we are challenged directly or our beliefs are challenged. What would it feel like to open up instead? A simple practice for this is breathing into our heart through difficult feelings and sensations.

3. Creativity

"It enabled me to see that risk-averse language had become part of my daily vocabulary practice. It also got me thinking of better ways of using language that helped children to manage risk by themselves and for themselves." **Sid Mohandas (2021)**

Sid reflected upon how a four-years-old child's response to the language he used for safeguarding supported him in finding helpful ways for children to manage risk.

With this in mind...

- Reflect upon the language you use with your child or the children in your care. Are you helping or hindering their physical development, their need for autonomy and self-confidence?
- Create a spider chart of language of "expansion" you can use with your child, to invite them into care, observation and self-responsibility to keep themselves and others safe.
- If your child is able to read and write, invite them to join this conversation and in the creation of this chart.

Share your thoughts...

I would love to hear your thoughts, so feel free to share them via any of the following ways to the Montessori Mission community:

- Email me sayhello@enrichingenvironments.com
- Tag me @enrichingenvironments and use the hashtag #montessorimission on Instagram & Facebook

Work book

Can you answer the 10 questions yourself?

1. What does Montessori mean to you?

2. What was your first light bulb moment on your Montessori path?

3. In what ways does Montessori enrich the work that you do?

4. When was the first time a child taught you something about yourself that you weren't aware of? (either through a direct interaction or an observation of them)

5. When was the last time a child taught you something about yourself that you weren't aware of? (either through a direct interaction or an observation of them)

6. When was the last time a child caught you out of integrity, and questioned you on it?

7. How did you explain yourself afterwards?

8. What is your favourite Dr Montessori quote?

9. What is your deepest desire for Montessori in the future?

10. What do you see is your role in achieving this desire?

Image: *Olivia and Harry's first cuddle - March 2017*

Epilogue

Whether you stumbled across my social media post, listened to one of my great guests on the Podcast series or we have worked together, I am so grateful that you are here now, having finished this book, the written account of the amazing, joyful and soul-satisfying Montessori Mission Podcast Series..

I hope that reading the fascinating stories contained in these interviews has given you a snapshot of the richness, and possibility in Montessori Education, Montessori Parenting and a Montessori way of life.

We all have an opportunity to mould a more peaceful, just and harmonious world; and from these rich interviews I seek to gift you with the following 10 simple and deliverable steps in order to bring a Montessori mindset and way of life into your homes, schools and communities:

1. Know that your child is immensely capable, even from the earliest days, weeks and months of their life.
2. Prepare your home environment with this in mind, place everything that they need to be autonomous accessible at their height.
3. Observe your child, their interests, their passions, what lights them up, what brings them joy. Knowing what brings them joy is a powerful gift of connection and validation.
4. Be there in the moment with your child when they accomplish something for themselves, observe their reaction and feel their intrinsic joy in their achievement, prior to offering praise.
5. Hug a tree daily with your child, feel the strong connection to Mother Earth and the sense of interconnectedness of all life on earth through this. Embrace nature as our greatest teacher.
6. Celebrate your cultural heritage and its richness. Give your child the gift of being able to see themselves, and see the outside world by offering them 'a mirror and a window'.
7. Trust your child, trust yourself. Honour your inner wisdom as a parent, Educator or caregiver.

The Montessori Mission, by Charlotte Awdry

8. Practise playfulness, hardly anything is a serious teaching moment!

9. Expand into more love; love and acceptance for yourself. The more we love and accept ourselves, the more we are able to offer these gifts to others.

10. Be kind and compassionate to yourself, being a parent is tough. We will uncover wounds that we did not know that we had. We all make mistakes, say and do things we regret. We are human! Embracing mistakes as part of our learning journey, practicising radical-self compassion (rather than covering ourselves in shame) and repairing after we make these mistakes is how we grow from these experiences.

Call to action:

Please spread the word, tell others about the possibilities of Montessori Education; much work has been done in recent years to diversify however there is such vital work to be done in making Montessori accessible to all.

Absorbent Mind

The unique quality of the human mind, most acute from birth to six, when the child learns by absorption and synthesis of stimuli from the environment.

Adaptation

Characteristic ability of all human beings to adapt to new experiences, conditions and circumstances of life. It is inherent in Montessori's notion of Cosmic education, and is an integral part of her evolutionary perspective.

Auto-didactic

Term used by Montessori to describe the qualities of the Montessori learning materials which enable children to teach themselves.

Conscious Absorbent Mind

The second stage of the Absorbent Mind, usually associated with the beginning of nursery education because the child is able to express basic needs through language and is capable of independence in dressing and personal hygiene. The child's ability to control his/her inner urges develops gradually, and the child begins to demonstrate the ability to use his/her will and demonstrate emerging awareness of socially appropriate behaviour. One of the two sensitive periods, characteristic of the Conscious Absorbent Mind, highlights the social aspects of life when the child is able to absorb and mirror social mores of his/her culture, and when awareness of the needs of others gradually emerges as the child de-centres. This sensitive period is closely linked with the child's normalisation, which is often referred to as the "socialisation process". During this stage of his/her life the child becomes conscious of the nursery community - Montessori refers to this as the cohesion of the social unit. The sensitive period for refinement of the senses is also evident at this stage of the child's life, and is supported by the use of sensorial materials which scaffold the development of the child's conceptual understanding of the world and the emerging ability to organise and classify information, explore, and problem-solve. All these aspects of the sensitive period, combined with the child's growing language skills, significantly contribute towards the child's cognitive development and demonstrate the emerging creative thinking.

Control of Error

A device developed by Montessori which gives the child an opportunity to perceive his/her error as manifested in all activities which are designed on the principle of one-to-one correspondence. Older children have control cards which give them the opportunity to check the correctness of their answers in solving mathematical and grammar problems. The purpose is to foster a friendly attitude to error.

Cosmic Education

A key element of Montessori Elementary education; it underpins the delivery of the curriculum. Its key focus is the theory of evolution as explained in the Great Lessons. The Lessons highlight the on-going change within the Cosmos and the interdependence of all existence on our planet. Adaptability of all species is also considered, as is our responsibility for the future of the Earth and role of global citizenship. These principles of Cosmic education should be an essential component of the preparations of the teacher and should be shared with children of all ages through modelling (with the youngest children), discussion and debate with the older children. They provide direct links with the UN's Sustainable Development Goals and aim to promote Peace education.

Creativity

Relates to all opportunities given to children to explore, problem-solve, think for themselves and express their thoughts, feelings and ideas. It is inherent in all that the child does. It is perceived as the natural outcome of the child's learning in a Montessori setting because the child is given the opportunity to learn from the environment, along with sensitive support from an adult.

Cycle of activity

Describes any activity the child undertakes in a Montessori setting. It begins with a decision to do something, finding the activity either inside or outside the classroom (usually found on an open shelf for easy access), and engaging with it for as long or as little as the child needs to. The cycle is finished when the activity is returned to the shelf, ready for another child to use.

"Follow the child"

One of the foundational concepts of Montessori, following the child is to allow the child to experience and engage in activities that interest them. But more importantly, it means the adults resisting the urge to lead the child or place their own agenda/expectation upon them.

Great Lessons

The backbone of the Montessori classic Elementary (6-12) curriculum. They are the tools for the delivery of Montessori's vision of Cosmic Education. They explore the history of life on Earth, emergence of human beings, early civilisations and the history of written language and mathematics.

Horme

The inner drive which guides the very young child in his/her learning and development. Montessori also refers to the Hormic Impulse, which drives the child toward unpremeditated action and independence.

Human tendencies

The unique and genetic characteristics of all human species. Montessori includes orientations (in relation to spatial and environmental awareness and sense of order) gregariousness, adaptation, communication and imagination. These tendencies are manifested in children's Sensitive Periods.

Imagination

A unique tendency characterising the human species. Montessori believed that imagination is best cultivated through real experiences, as evident in children's spontaneous role play, when scenarios from daily life are re-enacted. She believed that contact with nature and sensory experiences are the best guide in supporting children's emerging imagination.

Imago dialogue

A simple path to restoring connection

and empathy, the Imago Dialogue is a unique and powerful communication tool originally conceived by Dr. Harville Hendrix and his wife, Dr. Helen Hunt, that has been utilised by thousands of couples for over twenty five years.

The Dialogue is built upon the premise that while we humans are designed to believe there is just one "reality" out there, (naturally the one we perceive), the truth is, each person has their own unique reality, their own legitimate experience of the world and any given situation within it.

Materialised abstractions

A term that Montessori related to the qualities of the sensorial materials which enable the child to establish conceptual understanding of the environment.

Mathematical mind

A characteristic of the human mind which is capable of organised logical thinking and classification of information. The sensorial materials available to children in Montessori settings cultivate these aptitudes and prepare the child for later study of mathematics.

Metal insets

The metal insets are part of the Montessori Language Curriculum. They are a learning tool used to prepare children for writing. They comprise ten flat metal squares that have two components, a pink frame, and a blue metal shape, cut out with a knob in the centre.

Nido

Nido (or 'nest' in English) is a calm, nurturing Montessori Community for infants, from around 12 weeks up to when they are walking. The developmental needs of the young child are met warmly and sensitively by caregivers as they learn to move, communicate, eat and drink independently.

Normalisation

This term does not imply that the child is abnormal. In the Montessori context it means that the child is provided with conditions which enable them to follow a natural/normal path of development. It is a process of socialisation during which the child grows accustomed to life at the nursery. If the conditions are right, the child begins to demonstrate the characteristics typical of every child who is given time to engage with the environment and develop naturally and spontaneously according to his/her individual rhythm and inner guide.

OFSTED

The Office for Standards in Education, Children's Services and Skills in the UK, a government organisation that inspects services providing education and skills for learners of all ages.

Orff Schulwerk I Diploma

Orff Schulwerk is "Music for Children", a way to teach and learn music using poems, rhymes, games, songs, and dances as basic materials. The Schulwerk was created by composers Carl Orff and Gunild Keetman in Europe.

Peace Education

Lying at the heart of Montessori pedagogy. Dr Montessori recognised the important role education plays in helping children understand their contribution to creating a more harmonious and just world.

Pink tower

Iconic and instantly recognisable piece of Montessori material. Offered in the Casa (three to six year olds) classroom as part of the sensorial area, it comprises 10 pink wooden cubes, in 3 different dimensions, the smallest being 1cm cubed, and the largest being 10cm cubed.

Planes of development

Stages of growth accompanied by their typical characteristics. Each stage is unique and essential for maturation, contributing to development in the next stage. There are three key stages: birth to six (the stage of the Absorbent Mind); six to twelve (the childhood stage); and twelve to eighteen (the adolescence stage). Each stage is subdivided into three-year spans.

Play

Often called "work" in Montessori settings because it contributes to the child's development. It is any activity spontaneously chosen by the child or a group of children which absorbs their whole being.

Sensitive periods

Times of special sensitivity to the development of skills essential for life. These periods fully absorb the child. They are not linear and usually overlap. Those which are most evident in the first three years of life are sensitivity to movement, language, acquisition of skills for organisation skills (order) and noticing small detail; whilst skills for refinement of the senses or developing social aspects of life are prominent in from about three years onwards. When these special traits appear, it is essential that they are nurtured and supported so that they reach their optimum level. When the sensitivity passes, the acquisition of these skills will no longer come as naturally to the child. Adults should look out for the signs of sensitive periods and provide an environment which will facilitate their attainment.

Social embryo

Montessori uses the analogy of a physical embryo because she sees both the social and spiritual embryonic stages as periods of transformation. The social embryonic stage is synonymous with the stage of the conscious absorbent mind (between three and six years of age). At this stage the child emerges as a social being with a keen interest in social conventions of his/her culture. The child also begins to be less egocentric and displays an ability to consider the needs of others and put them in front of his/her own. At the end of this period of socialisation (around the age of six), the child should be socially aware and enjoy being part of a group. In most countries this is the age when a child enters compulsory education in school.

Social Justice

Is placed at the heart of peace education. From the beginning of their experiences in Montessori settings, children are encouraged to be agents of change. Inherent part of this agency is introduction to and gradual understanding of solidarity, equity, justice and care for each other and the planet. In support of the principle of global citizenship, children are offered "mirrors" to reflect and understand their own experiences and "windows" to glimpse at and connect with experiences of children living in other cultures around the world.

Spiritual embryo
Sometimes referred to as a psychic embryo; this is the time when the child's unique spirit/personality emerges. It corresponds with the unconscious Absorbent Mind, during which the Horme drives the child's actions towards independence and sensitive periods emerge.

Three period lesson
An integral part of learning in the Montessori classroom introduced in the Casa age group for introducing new vocabulary and concepts to a child that involves three key steps: naming, recognition, and recall.

Unconscious Absorbent Mind
Corresponds with the child's first three years of life, when the child is driven by the hormic impulse, when his/her personality unfolds and the sensitive periods become pronounced. It is essential that the child is treated with the utmost patience, sensitivity and care during this first formative period in his/her life.

Volition/will
Relates to the child's will, which becomes evident toward the end of the spiritual embryonic stage. It is vital that children are given opportunities to manage their learning in an atmosphere of freedom which also contains some element of responsibility. Adults must be careful not to dominate young children's decision-making and not substitute the child's needs and desires with their own. Too much adult control is damaging to the spirit of the child and prevents the development of self-discipline which is the key to the socialisation of the child during the first six years of life.

Work
Perceived by Montessori as the totality of the child's efforts which contribute to the formation of a mature human being.

Work-cycle
A period of time (usually one and a half to two hours in Toddler Communities, two and half to three hours in Casa classrooms, extending to four hours in Elementary classrooms) during which the child has the opportunity to spontaneously engage with a wide variety of activities on offer in the classroom. These activities may be solitary, with a friend, in a small group of friends, or with an adult. The key is that the activities are decided upon by the child. Provided the well-being of the group is respected, the child is free to decide on what to do and with whom. This is possible because all the activities included in the favourable environment are beneficial to the child. The work-cycle is one of the key elements which contribute towards the child's developing self-discipline and socialisation.

Glossary provided by Barbara Isaacs.

Bibliography

Introduction: (1) Association Montessori Internationale (AMI). Headquartered in Amsterdam, the only Montessori Association founded by Dr Montessori and her son in 1929. www.montessori-ami.org **(2)** The Sustainability Institute, Lynedoch, Cape Town. Founded in 1999, it's an international living and learning centre teaching, exploring and applying ways of being that are restorative. www.sustainabilityinstitute.net **(3)** Mon Ecole Montessori school: Umm Suqeim & Jumeirah, Dubai. IG: @ monecole.me

Chapter 1: (1) Montessori, M, Education for a New World, Montessori-Piersen Publishing Company, The Montessori Series Volume 5, 2007. p69. **(2)** Leboyer, F, Pour une naissance sans violence, Éditions du Seuil, 2008. p. 55. **(3)** Christine Dixon IG @the_ordinary_ sacred - Internal Family Systems Educator and Educational Therapist

Chapter 2: (1) GuidePost Montessori - a Montessori schooling network in 80 campuses in the US and Asia. guidepostmontessori.com **(2)** Montessori, M, Montessori Speaks to Parents, Montessori-Piersen Publishing Company, The Montessori Series Volume 21, 2017. p21.

Chapter 3: (1) Montessori, M, Education and Peace, Montessori-Piersen Publishing Company, The Montessori Series Volume 10, 2019, p53.

(2) Montessori, M, Education and Peace, Montessori-Piersen Publishing Company, The Montessori Series Volume 10, 2019, p53.

Chapter 4: (1) Montessori, M, The Absorbent Mind, Montessori-Piersen Publishing Company, The Montessori Series Volume 1, 2019, p269. **(2)** Johnston, L.J & De Vito, J, Lifting Hearts off the Ground - Declaring Indigenous Rights in Poetry, Mennonite Church Canada, 2017, Article 34.

Chapter 5: (1) Montessori, M, Montessori Speaks to Parents, Montessori-Pierson Publishing Company, The Montessori Series Volume 21, 2017. p27 **(2)** Gibran K, The Prophet, Heinemann, 1974, p20.

Chapter 6: (1) Montessori, M, The Secret of Childhood, Montessori-Pierson Publishing Company, The Montessori Series Volume 22, 2019, p140.

Chapter 7: (1) Montessori, M, The Secret of Childhood, Ballantine Books, 1973, p215.

Chapter 8: (1) Lamothe, M, This is How we Do It, Chronicle Books, 2017

Chapter 9: (1) Montessori, M, text unknown. **(2)** The Black Montessori Education Fund. Birthed in 2020 out of the urgent necessity for healing from the trauma of racism that is negatively impacting Black children.

Chapter 10: (1) Standing, E.M, Maria Montessori Her Life and Work, Plume, 1998, p. 307.

Further information

The Montessori Mission Podcast

Each of the transcripts in these chapters are available as separate podcasts (audio and visual) on the 'The Montessori Mission' series - view them at IG @ enrichingenvironments, YouTube, Spotify, and ITunes.

Further information on the work of any of the guests can be found here:

1. JEANNE-MARIE PAYNEL M.ED
   IG: @jeannemariepaynel
   www.yourparentingmentor.com

2. AKSHATHA CHANDRAKANTH
   IG: @maanvi_and_me

3. NUSAIBAH MACADAM
   IG: @rumi_montessori
   www.rumimontessori.org

4. TRISHA MOQUINO
   IG: @indigenouscheerleader
   www.kclcmontessori.org

5. BARBARA ISAACS
   IG: montessorimusingsuk
   www.montessori-musings.com

6. AZIZA OSMAN
   IG: monti.play
   www.montiplay.com

7. PILAR BEWLEY
   IG: @mainly.montessori.homeschooling
   www.mainlymontessori.com

8. TATENDA BLESSING MUCHIRIRI
   IG: @montessorionwheels
   www.montessorionwheels.org

9. OCHUKO PRUDENCE DANIELS
   IG: @momahillschool
   www.momahill.com

10. SID MOHANDAS
    IG: @montistory.101
    www.themalemontessorian.com

The two following projects use Montessori education as a tool to serve their BIPOC communities, I invite you to support their invaluable work through amplifying their work and donating to their cause. 10% of the profits from this book will be divided between these two projects:

- **The Keres Children's Learning Center (KCLC)** (Chapter 4) is a non-profit educational organisation supporting Cochiti Pueblo children and families in maintaining, strengthening, and revitalising their heritage language of Keres. www.*kclcmontessori.org*
- **Montessori on Wheels** (Chapter 8) is the move-forward in Montessori education. Rooted in a revolutionary and liberatory approach, they provide young children and their families access to Montessori education. www.*montessorionwheels.org*

The Montessori Mission, by Charlotte Awdry

How to work with me

enriching environments

meeting children where they are

I am honoured to serve in the following ways:

Consultancy for:

- **Parents and other Primary Caregivers** passionate about following the natural development of their child and expanding their heart to the inner work that calls all of us as we seek to heal generational patterns.
- **Educators (Montessori or other)** looking to ground their practice, connect deeply with their team and the children in their classroom, allowing the soul of each child to unfold.
- **Homeschooling groups/Coops** seeking guidance on preparing nourishing spaces for several children and growing together with like-minded families.
- **Schools or Early Childhood Centres** dedicated to serving the children in their care in their evolution towards autonomy and self- direction, whilst cultivating a loyal Parent Community and empowering team members.

Online Courses

Montessori-at-Home: An Introduction to Enriching Environments - 6 weeks of online self-paced self-study comprising of videos, homework and affirmations. From connection to discipline, setting up your home to the importance of play, rich language to positive communication; this is an essential companion for parents on a Montessori journey. Only $99.

Workshops

Both online and in-person, check out my website for my latest workshops *www. enrichingenvironments.com/workshops*

Free Online Resources

I offer a wealth of free resources including video, audio and articles across Instagram, Facebook, YouTube, Spotify and ITunes: Articles and downloads *www. enrichingenvironments.com/blog*

Contact me via Instagram and Facebook: *@enrichingenvironments*

With deep thanks to...

The founding members of the original Enriching Environments Toddler Community; **Carla Haibi and Deanna Paolacci** whose faith in me was in the end stronger than my self-doubt.

My sister Sophie for her unwavering support; and her brilliant brain as a heart-centred entrepreneur. **My brother-in-law Martin,** who set something so special in motion when he designed the Enriching Environments logo back in March 2019. **Saraswati Nagpal,** an inspirational Educator, dazzling creative, and Olivia and Harry's godmother. **My parents,** Tony and Amber, my brother James and his wife Alina - for all for their love, support and encouragement with my Montessori career and this book.

My Montessori Mentors: Barbara Isaacs in London, Gayle Thomson in Cape Town, and Halima Barr in Dubai. **My 'Whale Aunties'** in Cape Town: Michelle and Jacqui Graham, Marianna Van Niewerk, Claire Goffe-Wood, Emma Medell, Claire Howie, Gayle Thomson, Ibtesaam Gierdien. **Sara Dubois,** who trusted me with my first Lead Guide's role at Little Hands Montessori, Mowbray, Cape Town. **Houda Ramadan** (IG: @houdahub) whose social media presence and vision continues to inspire me.

The 10 Questions format of The Montessori Mission Podcast came from Nic Warner, (IG:@nicwarner). He is the creator of the 'Leaders of Men' Podcast, where he asks 10 men from around the world the same 10 questions.

Professional photography by the wonderful Laura McCone IG: @bylauramccone.

Behind the scenes...

Elizabeth Musangi: *Nairobi Kenya* - Podcast interview transcription. musangielizabeth30@gmail.com Find Elizabeth on linkedin.com

Beccy Hussain: *Toronto, Canada* - Editor & dear friend beccyhussain@gmail.com

Sarah Moore: *Amman, Jordan* - Editing & final proofing www.quran-connections.com

Sarah-Jayne Whitworth : *London, UK* - Book design & social media content www.sarahj-creative.com

Martin Barry: *Brighton, UK* - Logo design & front cover IG: @martin_barry_design

Thank you all!

Step by step, the fullness and expansion came,
Slow, long, difficult days, months, years, of patience.

There were demons in every dark corner to entice out,
lovingly unfolding each one from their giftwrap of shame.

Curious how in public they are not so shameful at all;
they are the demons in each of us.

Now, after this odyssey, the shadows are still there,
but I gladly take them by the hand,
hold them and embrace them.

Perfection is no longer the objective,
Vulnerability is.
Curiosity is.
Depth is.
Love is.

CHARLOTTE AWDRY

Printed in Great Britain
by Amazon

28881307R00110